Your Face Is The Mirror of My Soul

Your Face Is The Mirror of My Soul

Songs of Love and Delight

Songs of Loneliness and Terror

Sung with a Faithful Heart and a Determined Mind

As I Battled with the Angel in My Mirror

September, 2008 – September, 2009

Bird Neshama Trungma, Rinpoche

authorHOUSE®

AuthorHouse™
1663 Liberty Drive
Bloomington, IN 47403
www.authorhouse.com
Phone: 1-800-839-8640

First published by AuthorHouse   9/30/2009

ISBN: 978-1-4490-3087-2 (e)
ISBN: 978-1-4490-3086-5 (sc)
ISBN: 978-1-4490-3085-8 (hc)

Library of Congress Control Number: 2009909796

Printed in the United States of America
Bloomington, Indiana

This book is printed on acid-free paper.

Foreword

At first, I called the angel by the name Chogyam Trungpa, Rinpoche and myself by the name Bird Neshama Gelman. He was the teacher and I was the student, without question. However, as the warfare raged on, the angel began to address me by the name Trungma, and I soon found myself walking with a pronounced limp just like he used to walk with during his life, and just like Jacob, who became Israel, walked away with after fighting with his angel in the Torah (Old Testament) Book of Genesis.

During the course of battle, I came to understand that the real name of that woman who had spent her entire life fighting was

ISNOTRAEL

And that the beloved angel whom I met in my mirror ultimately ISNOTRAEL too. We were thus one and the same, or rather, none and the same. And although there was never really any war at all, nor was there anyone against whom to wage it, I nevertheless had no choice but to accept the sword which the angel placed into my hand.

My real name is Heart. Heart is all that there is, and at the same time, Heart is Nothing. Zero is Nero. The heart alone is invincible..

This book is dedicated to that warrior who can never be conquered, the Vidyadhara,, the Venerable Chogyam Trungpa, Rinpoche, my only Father- Guru. I am none other than he, the holy, beloved Trungpa tulku himself. At the same time, I am his beloved daughter. Finally, I am Absolutely Nobody.

Bird Neshama Trungma, Rinpoche
New York, New York
August 4, 2009

Trust in the Heart

Your whole life is a song about trust in the heart,
A song for living, a song for dying
That you cannot give up though you keep trying
Even if it keeps you crying.
It is a song which has been written upon your heart
With an indelible pen.
Your heart song is exactly how your life plays out;
It can never be otherwise.
Though you may try to run away from it,
You cannot escape from your heart song.
It will haunt you forever.
The only thing to do then is to sing it fully,
To dance it fully,
To dance your dance in space,
Celebrating completely and properly,
Bowing to your choiceless karma,
Making love to it as your choiceless lover
Who sings to you from inside your heart
And is never silent.

Jangchup Peta Paldren Chokyi (Bird Trungma)
Written on Wall of Isolation Cell, Boulder County Jail
Winter, late 1970's

Introduction

In the late summer and early fall of 2008, at 62 years old, I had finally come to believe that I might yet have the opportunity to sit under my vine and fig tree, live in peace and be unafraid. I had suffered an extremely painful and abusive childhood, followed by a difficult and tumultuous adult life. For most of the years that I lived independently, I kept my dwellings in a wretched state, which reflected my own inner wretchedness. But over the last few years, I had been taking good care of the space which I owned and lived in. It was a lovely, large studio apartment in an excellent doorman building in Washington Heights. Located on a quiet street adorned with many beautiful tall trees, less than a block from the Hudson River, its atmosphere was more rural than urban, with the songs of many different species of birds filling the skies and coming through my open window in the mornings. Everyone who visited me there remarked about how peaceful the environment was and how calm and happy they felt sitting in my home with me. I decorated the apartment a little at a time, partly due to financial constraints, but even more because of the slow pace of my emotional growth and the blossoming aesthetic maturity that came along with it. I did one thing at a time, first taking down the faded picture of nondescript, ghostlike characters inherited from my mother, and replacing it with a poster of a beautiful Bohemian woman with a Modigliani-like neck given to me by my friend Megan, which I had framed. I bought a stylish couch and a tall, elegant, multi-pronged silver floor lamp, whose prongs were so tall, they seemed like long silver arms reaching up to heaven. I called this lamp "my aspiration lamp." I made all of these wonderful changes, slowly but steadily, after I quit smoking. I have heard it said in the 12-Step Anonymous rooms that a person stops maturing at whatever point they pick up their addiction. My addiction was nicotine, and I had started smoking at the age of fourteen.

The most marvellous addition to my home soon after putting down cigarettes was a family of cats, who became my dearest loves. I named the first, a strong, handsome black and white male, Zisser Petunia. "Zisser" is Yiddish for sweet. Since right from the beginning, I sensed that Zisser was a highly intelligent and mature cat, I often joked around by referring to him as "the other adult in the house," and sometimes even called him "my husband." Then the other two cats became "our children." Yentl Flower, the second cat to join our household, was an independent and mischievous gray striped female. She looked like a tiger and was fearless, just like one, climbing wherever she wanted to on shelves all the way up to the ceiling, dangling from the highest ledges by a single paw. The last cat to join our family was Benjamin Dot, a small, shy, fragile male. Benjamin Dot's name was a consequence of his size, since he was as tiny as a dot, and for a long time, he was unable to gain any weight. He had no social skills in the beginning nor any idea of how to play like a cat. Yentl used her "feline womanly wiles" to socialize him. After that, Benjamin followed her around everywhere, trying to do whatever she did. In spite of being challenged by always remaining smaller than the other two and by being a bit of a slow learner, Benjamin was nevertheless a wonderful, good natured, sweet and gentle cat. Together these three animals filled my home with love. That might sound crazy to some people, raised in households with loving, caring human families (assuming there is such a thing), but since my own background was not so fortunate, I felt extremely appreciative to have this family of cats. The three of them never failed to gather around the door to greet me when I arrived home. Since Yentl, in particular, loved human food, I no longer had to feel sad about eating dinner alone, because she jumped right up on the table and served herself out of my plate. She liked whatever I cooked, even vegetables; like me, her favorite green vegetable was asparagus!

My cats never fought, since I made it exceedingly clear to them with abundant hugs and kisses and with the cheerful and generous sharing of food, that there was more than enough of both food and love to go around for everyone. Therefore, there was never any cause for them to fight.

Thanks to these wonderful, loving and gentle creatures, for the first time in my life, I did not feel lonely when I was home "alone," meaning without other humans. Instead I felt entirely relaxed, and it was this strong sense of safety I felt due to being in a loving environment, that allowed me to function well enough at home to finally be able to keep my apartment clean and neat, and then eventually to go beyond that and begin fulfilling my lifelong dream of becoming a writer. I started off by taking a couple of courses online with the Gotham Writers Workshop, just to get into the rhythm of writing and to develop some discipline. My first teacher was Barbara DeMarco-Barrett; she had just written a book called *Pen on Fire* in which she suggested that aspiring writers buy a timer and time themselves to write for a minimum of fifteen minutes daily, making the commitment to write for at least that amount of time each day no matter what. She believed it was much more important to develop the habit of writing regularly, if even for only a short period of time, than it was to write for five or ten or twenty hours straight, and then not touch a pen or keyboard again for six months. I quickly picked up the discipline of daily writing, and was soon able to write on my own every day, without the need for a teacher to hand me assignments or provide reinforcements by remarking about the excellent quality of my work. Besides helping me to become a professional writer, this exercise and the new attitude also taught me to become a more mature person. At first, I used to set my timer for fifteen minutes before I began to write, but after it went off, I inevitably ignored it and continued to write for another hour or two or three. Therefore, I pretty quickly dispensed with that tool. There was one situation in which the timer came in handy, though. That was during those times I came home late after a long day or woke up early after little sleep. Under those conditions, I definitely was resistant to writing, so I used the timer to trick myself into it, setting it for fifteen minutes and promising myself to stop after the timer went off. That usually turned out to be a lie, since once I got started on a piece, I could barely pull myself away from it. I only allowed myself to be "tricked" in this way because I love to write, so I pretended to be fooled.

As soon as I developed a little confidence, I went to work writing a memoir about my life as a student of the Buddhist guru, Chogyam Trungpa, Rinpoche, who was, himself, a gifted poet and prose writer. I worked every day for nine or ten months and got as far as page 650. These were well written pages, since it is not my habit to write a first draft and then edit it afterwards, but to do most of my editing as I go along. During this period of my life, I also began teaching expository writing courses part time as a college adjunct. Teaching English had been another lifelong dream of mine. I was obviously a late bloomer. Having been raised in a family that was entirely insane, I had a lot to overcome.

Then suddenly everything came to an end. Writing my memoir ended, playing with my cats ended, decorating my apartment came to an end and it was placed on the market for sale. My seat under the vine and fig tree vanished, and instead, I found myself seated on a plane bound for Nepal. I did not complete the memoir which was my heart's commitment and my joy to write, but threw its precious pages into the incinerator to burn. The next year was spent sitting in hotel rooms in Asia, and later Europe and America, writing poetry. I had not written any poetry since I was a teenager and had no inkling that I still possessed this skill.

My style of dress changed as well; I went from slacks and low cut blouses with big earrings and makeup to the yellow and red robes of a Tibetan Buddhist nun. The fact that I had no desire to make these changes did not impact upon my behavior. Thirty years earlier, I had fallen in love with the Tibetan Buddhist guru Chogyam Trungpa, Rinpoche, and had offered him my body, speech and mind in a spontaneous act of devotion. At the time, I had not yet acquired any tantric vocabulary with which to conceptualize, either for myself in my own mind, or for the sake of explaining to others, what was happening to me. Nevertheless, that was exactly what occurred.

When the Tantric Buddhist tradition speaks about devotion to the guru, this devotion they are talking about is nothing other than a high-falutin' word for love.

But, of course, it takes love to figure that out.

To love means to give oneself over completely. The giving over of oneself to the beloved guru and the taking up of samaya bondage are neither myths nor metaphors. The root of the word *samaya, maya,* means illusion. It is through the relationship of samaya bondage that the guru leads the student to liberation from the world of illusion. Samaya bondage is at least as real as everything else in the illusory world. To me, it is much more real than the computer I am using to type this book. It is by far more real than the fingers that are typing it.

It is only later after one begins practice that the real (not merely conceptual) understanding of giver and receiver, master and student, as one comes about.

This recounting in the form of poetry of one small segment of my spiritual journey, begun decades earlier during the Flower Child Era in San Francisco, opens in October 2008 and concludes almost a year later, shortly after my return to New York from McLeod Ganj in India. The verses belong to a class of poetry known in the Tibetan Buddhist tradition as *vajra dohas* – spontaneous songs arising in the mind which express realizations that occur as one travels along the journey of Buddhist practice. The main purpose of writing dohas is to help and encourage other spiritual practitioners, especially Buddhist practitioners and yogins of the future.

In my own case, however, I came by the realization of Absolute Truth , (and by that I mean having stuck much more than my big toe into the ocean of experience), shortly after writing the last doha. The understanding that there are neither any practitioners requiring encouragement nor any teachers needed to help them (that includes the one whom I perceive to be looking back at me from my mirror) was painful and confusing for some time. All of those whom I perceive to exist, with whatever label they happen to be wearing, whether student or teacher, are not only unreal, but furthermore inseparable from one another, joined forever throughout the non-existent, yet experientially real, march of time. That is because, obviously, it is impossible for a multiplicity of Nothing to exist. Zero remains zero, no matter what number it is multiplied by.

Moreover, because there are no actors, there can be no actions. This realization is what is known in Mahayana Buddhism as *the threefold purity:* no actor, no action, no acted upon. Once having realized this (again, nonconceptually), it was only too easy for me to slide down from the mountain peak which my egotism had labeled wisdom into the dark pit of nihilism and the depression that came along with it. Since there is nobody to read my dohas, why bother writing them?

Since there is no one to benefit by practice, why bother even getting up out of bed? This depression was all the more acute due to the fact that I was predisposed toward it, even prior to any thoughts or realizations about Emptiness. Thus I made much ado about Nothing, and spent a great deal of time worrying about it, hiding from it, and trying my best not to think about it. The result of all of those attempts to avoid the anxiety-provoking thoughts about Emptiness was that I sometimes forgot about the necessity of living in a practical manner and taking the sensible, middle path approach between existence and non-existence, which was professed by those Madyamika philosophers whose ideas formed the backbone of Tibetan Buddhist teachings, at whom I had secretly snickered while attending the Buddhist seminary, mentally labeling their position professing neither existence nor non-existence as "a big cowardly cop-out." Now I found myself in a position which demanded I change my attitude. The only way to climb out of the pit was to keep the Bodhisattva vow I had taken years earlier, made when both feet were solidly planted on Relative Truth's shore, and work for the liberation of all sentient beings – those who were neither existent nor non-existent!

This decision and the behavior which followed it provided an adequate antidote to my depression. In working hard every day to put this book together properly and get it published, I rose up out of the abyss like a phoenix rising up out of the ashes.

Since then, I have been blessed with increased knowledge about Absolute Truth, and that knowledge has made the thought of it less frightening. The truth that nobody is ultimately real does not negate the possibility of joyfulness. Self-existent joy requires no certificate of ownership. My Bodhisattva name, which was given to me by my root guru, Chogyam Trungpa, Rinpoche, is *Jangchup Chokyi*. The translation of that name into English is *Dharma Joy of Enlightenment*.

And while the Nirmanakaya Buddha, Chogyam Trungpa, was but my lens through which to view Truth in a form that I was capable of seeing it, and he was, in that form, himself not ultimately real, nevertheless he was also not a liar . Therefore, in spite of his having clearly stated, "There is no guarantee because there is no guarantor," I cannot resist taking the name he gave me as a promise which comforts me whenever I begin to become too frightened. That happens occasionally, in spite of my understanding that the big lie of ego is much more frightful than the truth is.

I am one hundred percent, one thousand percent, even one million percent delighted to present this book of dohas, published for the enjoyment and edification of whomever is inspired by karma to discover it and to pick it up and possibly even become absorbed by it. As far as my own benefit is concerned, I certainly prefer feeling joyful to feeling miserable. I have found over the course of my journey that a great deal of joy comes about as a result of making oneself useful to others. Therefore, for the present moment, I have chosen to set theoretical considerations aside and offer this book – even if it is to No one.

Happy reading! Blessings to all!

Bird Neshama Trungma, Rinpoche
July 26, 2009

A Letter To His Holiness
The 17th Gyalwang Karmapa,
Ogyen Trinley Dorje

January 18, 2009

Dear Holiness:

Thank you so much for this audience today. It is amazingly wonderful that karma should bring me here to you, in such a beautiful place as Dharmasala. I am 63 years old and have never before had the good fortune to have the opportunity to travel. Now I have not only traveled across the planet, but to heaven itself!

What I wish to share with you is that I first became a student of the Vidyadhara, the Venerable Chogyam Trungpa, Rinpoche, thirty years ago in San Francisco. I practiced shamatha meditation and took classes in basic Buddhism at the Dharmadhatu for many years, but the Vidyadhara would never allow me to go to his seminary to begin ngondro practice. Thus, I did not even begin ngondro until 2003, when I attended the Shambhala seminary with the Sakyong Mipham, Rinpoche. One of the understandings which has evolved from my path is that external ritual and ultimate real meaning are not always the same. The Vidyadhara became my guru, the master of my heart, the moment I first laid eyes on him. That was at a ball thrown by Vajradhatu back in the 1970's. The Vidyadhara, who was a tiny man, walked into the ballroom surrounded by a group of tall kasung. When the circle of kasung opened up and I saw the Vidyadhara* standing in their center, I thought, "He is the face of the flower, and they are the petals." I offered him my body, speech and mind right on the spot, without even knowing those words, without knowing that such a concept existed or having any Vajrayana **education at all. The real Vajrayana practice is to love the guru – that is it. All of the "fancy practices" – the sadhanas and special yogas, etc. are just ways to open the students' hearts so that they are able to experience this love, and in loving the teacher, to spontaneously let him in, even without realizing it. The amazing reality – that the mind of the guru can be mixed with one's own – soon leads one to realize ultimate truth – there is no one to be let in and no self to let anyone in. My fellow Dharmadhatu/Shambhala students looked down at me for years, because everybody came and went to seminary and went on to "bigger and better things," while I always remained behind, "the poor little shamatha girl who never got promoted." I saw myself that way as well. I didn't understand that this was my real Vajrayana path – the path of love and a broken heart. The whole situation was excruciatingly painful. One day a young woman who first joined the Dharmadhatu the same year I did and had gone to seminary years earlier, asked me jokingly "And when are you going to seminary, Sandra?" as she laughed and slapped me on the back. That was only one of many times I hung my head and went home from the dharma center crying.

My second contact with the Vidyadhara was that same year as the ball, during the same International Dharmadhatu Conference. I approached him at an exhibit of his flower arrangements in Denver and said, "You are so wonderful, sir!" His answer to me was "Look into your own mind." He just said that one sentence; then walked away. I felt so disheartened, thinking "Although I love this guru so much, he obviously doesn't care for me at all!"

I would like to say that perhaps Chogyam Trungpa looked to some people like the Guru Bari, the wealthy and arrogant contemporary of the *great yogin, Milarpa.*** He lived well and encouraged his students to do the same. He charged a good fee for his courses. He was chauffeured from here to there all of the time, and had students serving him elegant meals on fine china, as did Guru Bari. He owned a diamond business by the name of Triple Gem Jewels. In remembering my life and his life, which took place in a dream, that was the face I saw him present to the world. At the same time, it seemed to me that he was really someone different underneath the surface. I saw a Chogyam Trungpa who was the embodiment of Milarepa, of Father Marpa, of Naropa and Tilopa.**** In my heart, I became Peta Paldren, Milarepa's sister, and Chogyam Trungpa became the same Father Marpa to me as he had been to my brother. Thus the rejection for so many painful years. In the life story of Milarepa, Marpa rejected him over and over, beating him for just daring to step into the classroom, and working him until his entire back became one stinking, infected sore, oozing with pus and blood. The Vidyadhara and I related in a manner which was not very different from that, although we enacted a modern, Western version of the story. I am attaching a short, biographical essay entitled "The Misinterpretation of Karma as Psychopathology" at the back of this book which explains that statement in more detail. I am also working on a full length memoir entitled How I Became Trungma: Practicing the Buddhadharma Without Credentials, which will be completed in the near future, if karma allows.*

The last item in this offering book is an essay about global warming. I understand that you are very concerned about the environment. The essay, called "Creating a Team to Change the Theme of the Dream from a Planet Heating Up to a Planet Cooling Down" suggests a very Mahayana oriented project which Buddhists may wish to undertake and which you may wish to support.

Currently I have a visa allowing me to remain in India until April 11th. I would love to remain here on a permanent basis and perhaps be of some service. One idea I thought of was to open up a Karma Kagyu Center oriented towards westerners. Another idea has to do with finding some way to resurrect the lineage of women Karma Kagyu practitioners which I understand existed in the past. As you will see from reading these dohas, it has been extremely frustrating, painful and anger provoking for me to have to turn to all males/monks for permission and ordination to become a novice nun. As things are now, if I live long enough to go on to become a full bhikshuni, I will have to go to Hong Kong to a different lineage entirely to receive this ordination. My wish is become a full fledged monastic in the Karma Kagyu lineage, just the same as any monk. My wish is for other women who come after me to be able to become full fledged Karma Kagyu monastics – and yoginis. I see no reason why this should not be the case, why this cannot be made to happen.

I will telephone your private secretary, Lama Phuntsok, shortly, after you have had a little time to look over this material, in order to request a private meeting with you. I hope that you will be willing to meet with me, and that you will instruct him accordingly. In the meanwhile, I have volunteered to work with the organization Gu-Chu-Sum, and have begun teaching classes there as of yesterday. In this way, I will be able to help others, and perhaps help myself at the same time by gaining a reference which could help me remain in this country. I have also volunteered to do editing of translations through Volunteers for Tibet. My former profession before leaving New York was freelance writing and editing. This is work which I am passionate about; it is not just a job for me. Needless to say, I would be delighted and honored to provide editorial services for you or for your staff.

Should you wish to reach me before I contact Lama Phuntsok, you may e-mail me at chokyijangchup3@gmail.com. I am staying in McLeod Ganj

at a guest house called Hunted Hill; however, it seems there is no telephone there which is available for guests to receive calls.
All of my blessings, love and honor to you, Sir,
Ani Jangchup Peta Paldren Chokyi*****

Notes for Non-Buddhist, Non-Karma Kagyu or Non-Shambhala Readers

*Kasung or Dorje Kasung – Guards, Protectors. *Ka* means command in Tibetan. Therefore, they are protectors of the guru's command, that is to say, protectors of the dharma. The Dorje Kasung were originally called "Vajra Guards" when established by Chogyam Trungpa, Rinpoche.

**A more advanced level of practice.

***Milarepa is considered to have been the greatest yogin in the history of Tibetan Buddhism and is one of the main foreparents of the Karma Kagyu Lineage, to which Chogyam Trungpa, Rinpoche, and through him, I am heir. Marpa was Milarepa's guru, who was also a great yogin, and who is also considered a Karma Kagyu foreparent.

****All great yogins and founders of the Karma Kagyu Lineage.

*****The name I used as an ani (nun).

To His Eminence
Jamgon Kongtrul, Rinpoche

Bravado is not my style these days.

Though in the past, I used to march into a room with the foolish
confidence of an indoctrinated storm trooper,

These days, my behavior has grown gentler.

It is not that I have become wiser.

It is merely that karma has played itself out.

This evening, I do my work by candlelight rather than by flashing
neon.

I touch-and-go, touch-and-go, like my father-guru taught me

Rather than grab and shake red-faced, or blast advertisements by
bullhorn.

My father-guru shared his experience with kind simplicity rather than
by issuing imperatives.

He did not press heavily upon his pen, creating big black letters, big
ugly warnings, sentences with exclamations to frighten people.

Still, what he shared became written upon my heart.

The dharma flows in my veins.

The dharma is at my fingertips as I write.

It is the dharma which writes.

This is because of the love of my only father-guru,

Who has encouraged me to share this with you today.

With love and blessings,
Jangchup Peta Paldren Chokyi
1-16-09

Part One
New York: 10/8 – 10/18/08*

The night passes slowly when you've got a pain in your back and can't
sleep.
You can try counting sheep
Or drinking another cup of coffee.
You can plan for the future,
Imagining this or that.
You carry the past with you
Wherever you go,
Even in a dream.

Trungpa

I don't love him
Or I do.
I'm a Tibetan poet
Or a Jew.**

It doesn't matter.
I follow my feet
Wherever they lead me.

* * *

I take refuge with the Three Jewels*** in a dream,
As a poet, as a sage, as a queen.

Notes to Assist Non-Buddhist or Non-Karma Kagyu or Non-Shambhala Readers

*The book opens here because it was during this period that I began
to strongly experience my inseparability from the Father- Guru and
the sense that I had to sell my apartment and travel to Nepal to seek
ordination as a nun.

**Refers to the same phenomenon of inseparability from the Father-
Guru, who was Tibetan. My own background is Jewish.

***Taking Refuge with the Three Jewels is the name of the ceremony
in which one formally takes on Buddhism as one's spiritual path
(or in more traditional Western terms, converts to the" Buddhist
religion"). The Three Jewels are the Buddha, the Dharma and the
Sangha. The Buddha refers not only to the "historical Buddha,"
who was the Indian Prince Siddhartha, but also to the wisdom

or enlightenment within one's own heart, which is not any less than that of the historical Buddha. In Vajrayana Buddhism, one's guru is considered (and should be treated as) a living Buddha. It is through devotion to this living Buddha that one realizes one's own enlightenment or Buddhahood. The second refuge source, the *dharma*, simply means the Buddhist teachings. *Dharma* is also sometimes defined as "things as they are." These two meanings are considered to be the same. The third refuge source, the *sangha,* is the community of Buddhist practitioners. In Vajrayana Buddhism, the guru is said to embody all three "jewels" or sources of refuge.

• • •

When the voices in my head
Tell me to drop dead
It doesn't matter.
I do my practice,
Eating my cereal
And tying my shoelaces.*

• • •

I tried to suck in my brain.
It was in vain
And just made it rain.**

• • •

Dr. Freed,
Dr. Freed,
I plead,
Give me some speed.
He agreed.
It led me to heaven
And was really swell

Until I fell
Down into hell.***

Notes for Non-Buddhist, Non-Karma Kagyu, and Non-Shambhala Readers

*In both the practice of meditation and the post-meditation experience, many different thoughts go through the mind. One deals with them by first acknowledging them, and then returning to the task at hand. In meditation, the task at hand is mindfulness of the breath; in post-meditation, it is whatever what one happens to be doing, whether it is washing dishes or tying shoelaces, etc. Thus, the meditation instruction is to be aware of thoughts without dwelling on them.

** The first goal of meditation is to develop awareness of one's thoughts and an attitude of friendliness toward them. In that way, one develops friendliness toward oneself. On the other hand, the attempt to "suck in the brain" or fight with one's mind, is a way of being cruel to oneself. This behavior certainly does make it rain!

***The dharma teaches that dwelling in the "god realm" inevitably leads to a big fall down into hell. One reason is because we lack awareness of the surrounding suffering. The cost of this "blissful ignorance" is the development of an extreme rigidity or narrow-mindedness. In this rigid state, the mind is unable to handle any stress or hint of negativity, so when something unpleasant inevitably arises in the course of life, we wind up crashing down into the hell realm. While all of us visit the god realm from time to time, (e.g. come home from work, kick off shoes, turn on loud music, lie down on the couch, call up for Chinese take-out instead of cooking….) it is one thing to visit there occasionally, but another to try to turn it into a permanent home.

Shadow Boxing with the Father Guru in Starbuck's (Observing an Old Friend)*

She sits in the coffee shop reading her book,
Looking up,
Looking back down,
Looking up,
Looking down,
Reading,
Bleeding,
Pleading,
"Please, Mister,
Please, Sister,
Please Anyone-at-All,
(But the more credentials the better)
Pay attention to me."

She fixes her hair,
Curls her curls,
Twirls her twirls,
Wiggles her foot,
Wiggles her toes,
Wiggles her nose.
"Please, Mister,
Please, Sister,
Please Anyone-at-All,
(But the more credentials the better)
Pay attention to me."

Maybe a doctor,
A lawyer,
A millionaire.
No, a millionaire wouldn't be fair.
He's got to be an intellectual,
Although money does matter.
Maybe he'll be a mad hatter.
We'll sit and we'll chatter.
I'll fix him a wonderful batter
If he just has the right credentials**
And pays attention to me.

Can it be?
Does he see?
He looks at me!
She'll be my friend
Till my dying end.
We will defend,
And extend,
And expend
All of our energy
On confirming each other's existence.***

Is it true?
He looked at you?
Did he tease?
May I have your autograph, please?****

You are great.
You should be our leader,
My reader,
My bleeder,
My pleader.

She'll take a lover,
Or a friend,
Or anyone at all.
Please just sit at my table, Mabel.*****
Isn't life a ball?

I will defend******
To the very end
My right to write poetry.

Notes to Non-Buddhist, Non-Karma Kagyu and Non-Shambhala Readers

*The old friend was both a woman sitting "out there" named Karen and an old friend sitting in my mind named Sandra (my birth name). Karen's behavior mimicked exactly what my own had been years earlier.

**"Right credentials" is defined differently by different people. For some it means a lot of money; for others, it means the right Ph.D., for some elite few, it might mean having been born into a family with the right aristocratic name, etc.

***The Buddhist teachings on egolessness and emptiness state that there is no absolute substantiality either to ourselves or to the world. However, a sense of existence arises in us as a consequence of relating to others; i.e. "I perceive that you exist by seeing you, talking to you,

21

etc. Since I am relating to you as a real, existent being, therefore, I must be real and existent myself. " Another example: "I love you, which proves I exist" or "I hate you, which proves I exist." In both cases, the real motivation is identical.

****This is based on a true story from Vajradhatu-Shambhala history. A female kasung (guard) by the name of Carol J. claimed that Trungpa Rinpoche made a pass at her while she was standing at attention on guard duty, and she was unable to resist bragging about it to everyone in the sangha (community). The result was that she became as popular as a Buddhist movie star overnight.

*****The invitation to "Please sit at my table, Mabel" is implicitly spoken by Trungpa, Rinpoche here.

******No matter what is demanded of me on the path, it will inevitably get done, whether I like it or not.. However, if it were necessary for me to give up writing, this would be the most terribly difficult and painful command I could receive, as there has never been a moment in my life from earliest childhood on that I did not dream of becoming a writer and did not believe that I ultimately would become one, no matter what obstacles I might face along the way.

Starbuck's

1.

He sits and he chews.
He's got the blues
Which he tries to muzzle
With a crossword puzzle
And a chocolate biscotti.

2.

Little girl dressed in pink.
She's Vietnamese, I think.
Just give her a wink,
Her father may think
I'm some kind of a fink.
Should I take a chance
On romance
And give her a smile?
We all linger here a while –
The father,
The girl,
And the woman who forgets to write poetry.

3.

She tries to curb her blues,
By reading the news.
She calls a friend,
The conversation comes to an end.
She's back where she started.

She drinks coffee with Splenda,*
But it doesn't mend her.
This poet who wishes she were dead,
Writes a few verses instead.

I try to tell her,
She's a fine fella.
For she is he and he is me
And I am you and you are we.**
Still, she knows nothing more
Than that her heart is sore
And the only act that can cure
Is writing poetry.

Writing poetry is an act of love,
So sang the saddest turtle dove.

_____

Notes to Non-Buddhist, Non-Karma Kagyu and Non-Shambhala Readers

*A calorie-free, sugar substitute.
**Only emptiness is real; we are the manifestations of emptiness based upon karma. In a way, it could be said we all have the same one name: "Karma." The notion of there being any real, individual, separate or substantial existent beings is founded upon confusion and is incorrect. Nevertheless, this misperception is not necessary always bad, since it forms the basis for our spiritual journey upon which confusion ultimately dawns as wisdom. This is what makes a life!

Part Two:

Welcome to Nepal 10/23//08 to 2/12/09

Namo* to the Ineffable.

There is no answer to a question which cannot be formed.

The father-guru is beyond any concepts of him.

Tonight I sit and enjoy a cool breeze, looking up at a sky full of stars.

My father-guru and I are inseparable.

This is my bittersweet joy and the blessing he gave me.

11-1-08

_____

Note:

This word is roughly equivalent to "Hail" or "Long live ..."

Trungpa XI

How can I ever thank the holy father-guru?
He forced me to do what I didn't want to do.
Did want to do.
Didn't want to do.
Did want to do.
Didn't want to do.
He blew my house down and forced me to become homeless,
A citizen of the world rather than a citizen of the small, square box
which I called my apartment.
How could he be so cruel?
I demanded to live like a fool.
He violated my rights.
He demanded I rise to the heights.
I offered him my body, speech and mind
When I was still blind.
He forced me to see.*
Woe is me!
He doesn't believe in democracy.**
Samaya is real.***
How does that make you feel?
Does it appeal?
But don't think twice,
It's alright, babe.****

11-11-08

Notes

*The guru removes the two veils covering the students' eyes, which
have caused his or her blindness. The first veil is the veil of ego; the

second is the veil of superstition about how the world works. An example of the veil of superstition is the belief that things happen just as a matter of circumstance, for totally "objective" reasons, with no relationship to the spiritual path. This is never correct.

**The guru is not a democrat. He or she is the boss, period.

***Samaya bondage in which one turns one's life over to the teacher, absolutely.

****The words are from a song by Bob Dylan.

Cat Woman in Kathmandu

Sad.

Can't think of a thing to write.

Lonely.

I call an old friend and it ends up tight.

Do blues abuse?

Does Jangchup choose?

There is a beggar in Kathmandu

Who crawls on the sidewalk without having any legs.

He crawls and begs,

Crawls and begs,

Crawls and begs

Without legs.

I wish I could buy him a cup of tea.

I wish I could offer him just an ounce of me.*

He is teaching me to see –

But what, I haven't learned fully yet.

Tomorrow morning, I'll pass him on my way

To get a cup of good American coffee,

And a plate of ham and eggs,

And I'll eat as he begs,

And I'll finish the eggs,

And I'll finish the ham.

Perhaps for lunch, I'll eat lamb.**

Does anyone choose?

Does Jangchup abuse?

Is Jangchup a witch?

Is she a bitch?

Is she a victim?

It is 4:30 a.m.

Time for bed.

Tomorrow I'll keep practicing.

• • •

Only Mind is here.

Mind is everywhere

And is free of conditions.***

The woman in Kathmandu is Mind.

The beggar in Kathmandu is Mind.

The ham and eggs in the American coffee shop are Mind.

She who thinks she must attain enlightenment for the sake of the
beggar in Kathmandu is blind.

Still, she is determined to enlighten herself out of existence in order
to prevent the beggar from starving.****

11-13-08

Notes

*Kathmandu was full of beggars everywhere, but they seemed
particularly numerous and desperate on one street which was always
frequented by Americans because of having so many American-
style restaurants and shops. There was even a Baskin Robbins ice
cream shop which I was very thrilled to discover on that street....,
until I learned that it was impossible to walk out of there holding
an ice-cream cone because one became immediately surrounded by
seemingly hundreds of adults and children holding out their hands
and crying. If I gave to one, a hundred more immediately joined

the fray. Soon I developed a very strong sense of being in a *bardo*, meaning a situation full of frightening characters who are not real. Traditional Buddhist literature frequently refers to the bardo in between death and the next rebirth; however, the experience of life (in between birth and death) is also a *bardo*. When one practices the dharma with a good guru, one begins to understand both oneself and others as unreal characters in a dream-like situation. That is because we mistakenly believe ourselves and others to be real and distinct physical entities, separate from Mind. Visiting this street became a type of bardo practice for me which was difficult and painful.

**The eating of lamb refers to the same issue. Lambs are beautiful, gentle creatures, who do not, however, exist in Absolute reality. To eat or not to eat? That is the question. To try answering it by thinking it through logically may well fail to provide a satisfactory resolution.

***Mind is another word for "Buddha-nature." It is a positive way of referring to emptiness and energy, which gives rise to all things – which are mental phenomena and not really *material* things, independent of the Emptiness-Energy of which they are manifestations. Although its ground is emptiness, Mind is at the same time rich and full. Because it is insubstantial, it is also unconditional, dependent upon nothing. The identification with this unconditioned Mind as one's true nature is the real meaning of enlightenment.

When I use the term *Heart*, it has the same meaning as Mind, which is the word traditionally used in Buddhist literature.

****In the above case, the illusory nature of the starving beggar becomes apparent. One needs to be careful not to use this teaching in a flippant way, which would result in an extreme lack of compassion. It is not okay to say about someone whom we see starving, "It's okay, because he/she doesn't really exist anyway" while mindlessly laughing and filling our own bellies full of food. In other words, it is not okay to use the dharma as just another justification for a lack of compassion. There is really no logical solution or formula guaranteeing "spiritual okay-ness." One has to behave gently and courageously at the same time, feeling one's way around these issues. Devotion to the guru allows one to have the necessary confidence to go forward in any situation.

Loneliness Street*

There is nobody here at all,
But the Lineage and I are one.**
A nun is a none.
I do not choose***
Whether to celebrate life or sing the blues,
Whether to practice or sleep,
Or fast or binge,
Or step out with a sense of humor,****
Or hide and cringe.
Nevertheless, a little friendship goes a long way.
The Lineage and I are one today.
And I do not slice it.
And I do not dice it.
And I do not splice it.
I take life as it comes,
Whether I reign or I slum,
Though I would rather shine,
A little friendship is just divine.

11-21-08

Notes

*This was written after first meeting Dechen, the daughter of the owners of the UTSE Hotel in Kathmandu, who are Tibetan Buddhist refugees there. Her warmth and friendliness, along with that of her mother, Dickee, was very comforting to me at a time when I felt totally isolated and depressed.

**Karma Kagyu Lineage of Tibetan Buddhism. As the student continues to practice, he or she develops the understanding that the Lineage is not separate, outside of herself or himself. Hence the student moves from the subjective position of a beggar to full Lineage membership.

***We do not choose, since there is no one to do any choosing. Rather, karma unfolds. Understanding and accepting this fact is sometimes referred to as "surrendering."

****Many years ago, in a group interview, I complained to Trungpa, Rinpoche very sadly, "I would like to work hard to propogate the Buddhadharma, but I am too shy to do anything. What should I do?" His answer to me was "Step out with a sense of humor." That was certainly great advice. If you try to practice the path without the ability to enjoy a good laugh, you will end up as dead meat!

Misunderstanding

This is how the dharma gets twisted:
"Get rid of your mind," they insisted.*
"Behave like a clone; don't go off alone.
We may throw you a bone
Or turn you into a stone."
I tried to cover my face,
Every hint of self to erase,
To carefully stay in my place,
The dharma not to deface.
I dutifully beat my breast
To show I was the best
At being the worst, so accursed
Yet at the same time, still genuine.
Though I never looked in the mirror,
Because I thought it would make me a sinner,
I saw my own hypocrisy,
And I took their teachings to heart,
And I pulled my innards apart.

The guru with the empty mind.
The guru with the full mind.
The guru who is everyone.
The guru who is no one at all.
The guru with the shining face,
Who did the world erase.
Her sangha was no one at all,
Yet they invited her to the ball.**

Yes, I would love to do this dance,

And take a chance on romance,

Said the very shining face,

Of the nun who did erase her face.

She was gone without a trace.

Was she here?

Was she there?

Was she a dear?

Or was she a wild bear?

You had better watch out for her claws,

Though sometimes, she has gentle paws.

This good news was written by the hypocrite who loves to write poetry.***

11/25/08

Notes

*The understanding here is that "they" were projections of my own confusion. The major misunderstanding I had for many years was that I had to be some kind of a "generic Buddhist" rather than just being honest and being myself; therefore, I suppressed demonstrating any kind of personality. This was what I now refer to as the behavior of ego, pretending to be non-ego. Ego has more to do with dishonesty than anything else. If a person enjoys applause, they need to develop the courage to get up and get it, not hide behind the dharma, using it like a mother's apron, lying and saying, "Oh, not me! I don't want any attention. I'm just a ...." Unfortunately, I have found that women often (though not always) suffer from this type of "neurotic egotism" worse than men.

**Neither the sangha nor I really exist; we are karmic hallucinations. Nevertheless, in this hallucination or dream of a life, I was invited to the Vajradhatu ball, where I met the guru. This was at the Pan-Dharmadhatu Conference in the 1970's, mentioned earlier.

***Humorous commentary implicitly made by the guru.

Homecoming

Long Western-style raincoat
Rolled up into a ball
Thrown into a corner of the closet floor.
Western-style purse, formal, with clips and zippers,
Next to it, unused.
Will they ever be used again?
To ask the question is futile.
The overcoat's pockets are empty.
The purse is empty.
The answer to the question is empty.
One night, I will take a taxi from Kennedy Airport in the rain
And I will watch the raindrops as they move along the window
And feel the teardrops rolling down my cheeks.
And teardrops
And raindrops
And teardrops
And raindrops
Will merge, and it will be as in a dream.

11-28-08

Letter to Elsie on the Four Noble Truths*

Before the holy dharma, I worshipped cows.**
I thought I was Other,***
That a cow was my mother.
I thought I was born.
Was full of self-scorn
And full of self-pity
And full of fear
Of a death that was empty
After a life of struggle in vain
Trying to beat up my brain.

There is no Other.
I have no mother.
There is no cow,
No hoe,
No plow,
No sweat of the brow.

Only dharma is here.****
It is perfectly clear,
Only dharma is here, my dear.*****

12-1-08

Notes

*Elsie the Cow was a character in an old, American advertisement for condensed milk.

**Historically, Hinduism, some of whose followers worship cows, preceded Buddhism. The historical Buddha, Siddharta, was originally a Hindu. Beyond that, the meaning here is that before practicing the dharma, we believe we are material creatures or things, subject to birth and death.

***After Buddhist practice, we see through this superstition; we are actually Mind, not matter.

****Dharma and karma are essentially the same word; we tend to talk about "dharma" rather than "karma" when looking at things from a positive or optimistic viewpoint. Since the teachings of the dharma are all about karma, there is really no difference.

Birds

I would like to write a poem without sadness.
How can I do that?
The sky is filled with birds headed home to eat their dinner.
I will eat mine too.
The world is too beautiful and its holiness is too profound
When I reflect on it.

Should I want to be mindless like a bird?
They are not really there
Nor am I here.
Still I wish to be one of them.

In this dream, which is too lonely,
I am a fellow bird
Haunted forever by the illusion of separateness.

12-3-08

Ceremony at a Buddhist Hotel*

I had a terrible nightmare last night
In which I stood with a group of women who were all stooped over.
They put a platter in front of me and told me to eat,
And when I asked what it was, they said it was monks' left-over food.
"But I'm a nun," I said,
"Also dressed in yellow and red.
If a monk is such a special bird,
Please feel free to eat my turd.
I'll sell you two for a dollar."
But the women started to holler,
And they accused me of spiritual materialism.

I had a terrible nightmare last night
In which I lay in a hospital bed,
And a big, ugly rabbi with a cap on his head
Came into my room with a face that bespoke doom,
And bent over my head and said,
"Sandra, I'm Rabbi Elfenbeind, and I'm here to help you."**
But I told him, "If this is how you introduce yourself,
It is clear that you are here to help yourself
And not me.
How stupid can I be?
Get out of my room!"
And I chased him with a broom.***
But he accused me of having vanity
As a symptom of insanity,
And told me to discuss my egotism with a psychiatrist.****

I am a sinister minister,

Who dares preach a dharma of truth.

There is no other,

There is no mother or brother or teacher or therapist or president

Or any other kind of resident

Who can save you.*****

But if you want to pay me a lot of money,

I'll gladly pretend to be your honey,

And you can pretend to be my bunny.******

So, my darlings, serve me a good meal,

And maybe we'll strike a deal.

I'll save you some left-over food,

If I'm in the mood.

Ain't the dharma sweet?

Now try to cheat

And keep passing down the meat,

And keep whipping yourself if you must

Until you bust.*******

Cause I'm a very sinister minister,

A rabbi without an alibi,

A nun who used to be a bird.

Would you like to buy my turd?

Or as my father-guru once put it,

"Om grow up svaha."********

12-5-08

Notes

*This poem was written after participating in a ceremony for good
health at a Buddhist owned hotel, which was officiated by a group of

monks. The young woman who invited me said, "After the ceremony, we will have lunch. Since you are an ani (nun), you can have the honor of serving the monks, and then my mother and I will serve you." Although this sickened me, I attended in order to avoid giving offence, but did not participate in any serving or eating; instead, I remained in the shrine room meditating while the monks sat around the table eating their food and continued meditating all afternoon until the ceremony ended, at which point I left. This incident, which made the lack of equality between monks and nuns so painfully clear, sickened me during the entire time I was in Nepal. It was at this point that it became crystal clear to me that gender issues were at the heart of my path, rather than merely incidental to it.

**Sandra was my first name before I changed it legally to Bird. Notice that this rabbi's name, Elfenbeind, also has significance.

***His addressing me by my first name, while introducing himself as "Rabbi Elfenbeind" made it clear to me that he has entered the situation for the sake of his own ego, not for the sake of helping me. If people become rabbis or ministers or doctors or psychotherapists or anything else in order to feel superior to others, that is an excellent indication they should not be trusted, because they are only out for themselves rather than for the people they claim to be helping.

**** WARNING: Practicing egotism without a license is not only a symptom of severe psychosis -- it is against the law!! You may be fined or imprisoned if convicted!

***** and ******The truth is that no one can save anyone else. But if you go to a therapist and pay him or her a nice fee, he or she will pretend to be your protector, and you can convince yourself that you are safe, so long as the relationship lasts (usually, this means so long as your money holds out). Often so-called religious leaders play this role as well.

*******Passing down the good stuff to somebody else and pretending not to care for any of it for yourself is cheating because it is dishonest. The sentence "ain't the dharma sweet?" is my expression of rage over that dishonesty, both at the "bashful liars" and those who profit from their confused dishonesty.

********This was said by Trungpa, Rinpoche at a seminar in Los Angeles. It was a play on the mantra contained in the Buddhist "Heart Sutra," that goes "Om gate, gate, paragate, parasamgate, bodhi svaha." However, here he got down to the ultimate heart of the heart of instructions for the spiritual path – the very secret, esoteric imperative: grow up! I left this seminar with my homework assignment that I would spend the rest of my life working to fulfill.

Mao's Instant Noodles

I drafted a book of dharma poems in a notebook that read "Mao's Instant Noodles" on the cover.

I thought that was so hilarious,

I must be delirious.

If you would like an instant noodle,

You may turn into a poodle.

If you would like to be a poet or a person who has found your diamond heart,

Which has never been separate or apart

From everyone you ever loved or hated,

You must face the fear, my dear,

Come face to face with the terror of not being who you thought you were

And finding no easy answers.

Every question of dharma may be answered with a word that explains absolutely nothing.

But Mao's Instant Noodles can solve every problem of life.

If you want instant gratification,

Just shoot every person in the nation you don't like.

Force your enemies to take a hike.

Or just stay home and swallow a pill

And declare yourself mentally ill.

But if you would like to become a treat

To everyone you meet,

To become a dharma feast,

Rather than an ego beast,

You have to do the work

And not behave like a jerk,
Demanding easy answers
And instant gratification
And somebody else to hold your hand
And solve your problems for you.
It is much easier to swallow a pill
And declare yourself mentally ill,
Or swallow a Mao's Instant Noodle
And become a materialist poodle.*
But the truth will bite you back,
Either today or tomorrow:
You have to face the fear, my dear,
Of not being who you thought you were.
Only karma is here.
Only karma is here.
And the dharma offers no easy answers.

12-6-08

Notes

*It is always tempting, when the going gets rough, to take the easy way out. That kind of answer however, only works for the short haul, never the long haul. Ultimately, there is no way around doing the karmic work that must be done.

Tangerines and Tea

Empty-hearted.

No more poems to write.

The father-guru is real, yet not real.

Jangchup is real, yet not real.

Is there anything under the surface?

If I do not exist, why continue to live?

If you do not exist, why should I share the dharma with you?

Teacher and student ponder these questions as they peel the skins off

tangerines and enjoy cookies and tea together,

Although at the moment, only the tangerines and tea are real.

Perhaps cookies will be shared on another day.

In the meanwhile, Jangchup dreams of them.

12-10-08

Annette M

"Annette M is probably dead by now," I think to myself idly, sitting at my dresser table, finishing the last potato chips out of the bag. "I never really got to know her that deeply, but I remember her kindness in coming to my mother's funeral when I first joined the synagogue.* I was quiet and shy back then, so she must have assumed that my mother was shy and socially isolated too. She figured no one would show up to the funeral, so she came."

Annette seemed to me to be such a handsome woman; I followed her around like a puppy. She was never overtly unkind. I guess she just made the judgment that I was not in her same tax bracket or professional category. She let me hang out with her crew once in awhile, until one day in the Washington Square subway station, I kissed her goodbye. The kiss was so sweet, I couldn't resist asking, "Annette, will you marry me?" She didn't say anything, but her silence was a violent punch. I shrunk to invisibility. After that, we never hung out again. Somehow our schedules always collided, so we couldn't get together.

I saw her in the restroom of the Javitz Center on Yom Kippur,** wearing a beautiful white suit. She looked so tall and slim and stately. I greeted her, "Shana Tova!"*** and approached to give her a kiss, but she waved me off, saying, "I can't kiss you; I have a cold." A few minutes later, I saw her hugging and kissing her friends in the sanctuary. My chest swelled up, flooded with anger and tears, and I hissed to myself, "Drop dead, Annette! Go to hell!"

The last time I saw Annette M was ten years later, in the lobby of the New York Lesbian and Gay Center. She was sitting on a bench near the reception desk, waiting for a Lesbian Cancer Patients' meeting. We sat and talked and she told me that her cancer was spreading, and that her chances for survival were slim. "I'm sorry…if there's anything I can do to help…" I stammered, but she just answered, "We all have to die." She appeared strong, not teary at all. I was the one who excused myself to run out weeping.

All of this class garbage is so stupid. I really loved Annette. I wanted to marry her.

All of the rage about what never was nor could ever be is such a waste. I'm so sorry for cursing Annette that day. I'm so sorry for wishing her dead and sending her to hell.

Annette M is probably dead by now. My tears cannot change what is, what was, or what will be.

I wish her farewell.

12-15-08

Notes

*Congregation Beth Simchat Torah (CBST), the lesbian, gay, bisexual and transgender synagogue.
**The Jewish Day of Atonment, which comes at the beginning of the year.
***Happy New Year

Refugee*

There is a foreign flavor on my tongue tonight.
Boiled chicken gizzards with beans and vegetables I cannot name
Empower me to become a homeless refugee at home in her homelessness.
I manage to stomach it. It is at once awful and delicious.
I cannot run away.
I am in Nepal to stay.

I take refuge as a refugee from childishness.
I take refuge as a pilgrim fleeing skyscrapers, cement, and superior people,
Seeing earth for the first time,
Tasting it, drinking it, dissolving in it.
In this place of so-called inferiority,
I walk home on a dirt road and am amazed to notice that a chicken is
white and has yellow legs.
The chicken walks beside me; her skinny chick follows behind.
Mother and chick.
Mother and chick.
For an instant, I wonder if it isn't some trick
Of the eye, for life to appear so simple and holy.
What is happening to my mind here?
A cow with no complaints and no agenda meanders along the road
nearby.
I take lessons from everyone.

12-15-08

_____

Notes

*This poem and all of the following ones up to "Red Cross" were
written after moving into a house which I rented in the Sukadhara

residential district of Kathmandu. I had the notion that I might live there and turn it into a nunnery. However, I remained in the house only for a short period of time, quickly fleeing from an infestation of mice and other vermin. By the time I returned to the UTSE Hotel, both hands and arms were entirely covered with bites. I hid my arms from the hotel owners, Detchen and Dickee, for fear that they might not let me stay because they would worry that I was contagious and would infect the other guests. Fortunately, no one became ill, and the bite marks soon disappeared.

Nepalese Path

Yellow shirt,
Burgandy skirt,
Burgandy sash –
Very holy attire
In which to retire
All hopes and expectations.
The dharma is nothing if it does not bring happiness.
I worry about this and that – what he thinks and she thinks.
All of the rushing about in circles is a lot of baloney.
The pursuit is entirely phoney
From top to bottom.
I no longer care
About who is a peer
And who is superior
Or who is inferior.
Practicing the true dharma, free of credentials,
I step outside my door,
To find samsara's cure:
Fruition in the face of a baby goat.

12-20-08

Gopal
(The Handyman)

He thought I was alone in my home.
He swaggered in, drunk with his belief in his own superiority,
Some garbage about tobacco dribbling out of his mouth along with
sick saliva.
He chewed a mouthful of food as he spoke to me.
He opened my desk drawers without asking, as if the house were his,
Then informed me he'd be back within the next couple of days to fix
the shower he promised to fix last weekend.
This is my home. I pay the rent here.
All of this behavior is not okay.
I do not want to play
The helpless maiden and big mister man game.
Thus the game comes to an end.
This man is not my friend, nor am I his.
I am not his wife.
I am in charge of my life, and I do not want him in it.
This is my home, and I will not let him in it
Ever again.

12-21-08

Letter to Thrangu Rinpoche*

I went to visit Thrangu Monastery yesterday
In order to find someone to help me with my house,
To make some repairs and teach me how to pay my bills written in an unfamiliar language.
The monk who met me at the entrance handled me well.
The monk who wrote down my request handled me well.
The monk who saw me out handled me well.
I loved being handled so well, like a problem child.
I loved being held apart, like a piece of foul crap, to be poked at with a pole gingerly from a distance.
No one was rude in any way.
Afterwards, the monks all walked across the courtyard to the dining hall to get their evening meal.
It took me over five hours to get home on public transportation.
By the time I arrived, I was too sick to eat.
I am a woman.
I am a nun.
While the monks gather in puja** I shop for vegetables.
While they study logic and Buddhist philosophy, I negotiate a hard-to-light oven.
Unlike the men, I pay cash for everything.
Welcome to the Karma Kagyu Lineage.
Thinking about transplanting the Buddhadharma to the West?
Thinking about spreading the Buddha's message throughout the world?
I am a woman.
I am a nun in the Karma Kagyu Lineage.

I will also spread the Lineage's message in the world,
And that is the message I have to share.***

2

My father-guru must have been a nitwit
To send my tit
To get rid of the shit
And erase my face
In this barbaric place
And get rid of the lace
Which was nothing but a phony, hypocritical lie.
This Vajra Mahakhala**** with a pink ribbon
Will continue to be treated like a gibbon
Until she does.

3

She is done with me.*****
I, the father-guru
Have been fired by this Jew
Who sat in the dark
And just for a lark,
Threw slices of stale, Nepalese bread across the room.
"It's a special nun's exercise," she said,
"Throwing slices of bread.
In my spare time, I do stuff that's neat,
Like spitting at monks in the street.
Aren't I sweet?
I am a nun like my Uncle Herbie is the Queen of England!"

Thus this Vajrakhala flew
Together with her father-guru
Anywhere out of Nepal.

12-26-08

*Either this punk******
Is treated the same and equal as any monk
Or she's gone.*

12-27-08

Notes

*This poem and the next one were written in response to the same incident.

**group practice

***That the Lineage doesn't practice what it preaches, because it preaches that form is emptiness, (ultimate truth), but then discriminates on the basis of a person's genitalia (relative truth). People in the West who are not aware of the discrimination within the Buddhists sects in Asia should be made aware of it. Everyone (especially women) should be fully informed about these conditions before they decide to whom they should write a check and/or not write a check. When it comes to correcting wrong conditions, money makes the loudest speeches and is heard and responded to more effectively than any other speaker.

****Wrathful deity; the major protecting deity of the Karma Kagyu lineage. The idea here is that a Mahakhala with a pink ribbon is a wrathful deity who is unaware of her true nature and/or trying to hide it and pretend to be someone other than whom she truly is.

*****and****** seems to be recited by Trungpa, Rinpoche.

The Taxi Ride

I tried

To catch a ride

On the city bus

To return home from my preceptor's monastery in Boudernath to
Sukadhara.

The bus stopped

And on I popped

After the driver assured me it would take me to my neighborhood.

Instead I was given a tour of Kathmandu,

Of all the hidden, ugly places I wouldn't want to be stranded in.

I finally jumped off at Ratna Park,

Which was a place that I at least recognized.

I walked from Ratna Park to the Kanti Path

To try to catch a mini bus from there to Ring Road and to my home.

I walked from one stop to the next

Asking each driver, "Sukadhara? Sukadhara?"

But I became more and more vexed

And more and more desperate

As one after the other, they stared at me with a blank expression,

Then drove off.

I had only one hundred rupees with me, not enough for a cab,

And the sun was starting to go down.

I walked to Thamel, to the UTSE Hotel,

And there I borrowed one hundred rupees from the owner, my only
friend in Nepal.

I felt like hell.

It was more than five hours since I'd left Boudernath

On what should have been a ten minute ride.

When I stepped out of the hotel,

There was no one on the street and I could not find a taxi.

The few that went by were full.

When at last, I found a cab and got in,

I told the driver I would pay him two hundred rupees to take me home.

"What? Only two hundred?" he thundered,

"You've got to pay at least three!

Don't you dare cheat me!"

I opened the door and started to get out when he spat, "Alright, two hundred!"

I was shaking

And felt despicable,

Pathetic and poor.

After all, I was only coming from my spiritual mentor's home,

Why expect to be treated better?

Why expect more?

It was now black in Kathmandu.

There was no light anywhere,

And the cabbie drove around in circles, on rocky back roads,

Past foreign looking abodes

Which were wood and tin shanties.

He kept cursing.

I held my breath.

He drove me to hell.

On a street I did not recognize,

He announced, "Sukadhara! Inside or outside?"

Men stood in front of their shanties staring, as the cab rolled along.

"Inside or outside – what?

What do you mean?" I answered in a high, cracking voice which betrayed my terror and rage.

"Just take me to Sukadhara!"

The driver grunted.

After all, he was doing me a wonderful favor for only two hundred rupees.

He drove me on to a hill, where people stood waving sticks on the road.

"Sukadhara! Sukadhara!" I cried.

My mind went insane.

As the denizens of hell all waved their sticks on the black street

Where I was sure he would discharge me from my seat,

I gave him a blow job in my mind and then stabbed him a thousand times

Until all of Kathmandu drowned in a mixture of his slimy, diseased blood and cum.

Finally, he let me out in Sukadhara.

Whoever emerged from that cab was no nun.*

12-26-08

_____

Note

*Instead, it was the Vajra Mahakhala (sans pink ribbon). Thus, my father-guru's mission was accomplished via this exercise in terror!

Rinpoche

Money all spent.

I am broke.

Rage all petered out.

Were it not for thoughts about inequality,

I would be contented.

Were it not for inequality,

I would be content.

Everything is empty.

Both pride and shame are empty.

Still, isn't it better to live in the world with one's head held high?

House is quiet.

Clock on wall tics – tics – tics. It keeps me company.

Practice is good.

I, as Vajrasattva, recite – recite – recite the sacred mantra.

I become one with its words.

I need no other company.

I refuse to play the role of an ani – auntie – ani – Auntie Jemima.*

I am Buddha. Why pretend to be less?

If I am banished for refusing to conform, so be it.

I want to be a Rinpoche, not a Rinpoche's servant.

In this life-dream, I served the guru as a young woman with an open
and loving heart.

Many years later, I have found fruition as a mature practitioner.

Why pretend to be a girl?

Why play the role of a perpetual student?

Now is the time to teach.

If I have learned any dharma in my life,

Now is the time to share it.
"If I am not for myself, who will be for me?
If I am only for myself, what am I?
If not now, when?"**

12-27-08

Notes

* The term "ani" means aunt in Tibetan. Buddhist nuns are addressed as "Aunt" in Asia, just as Catholic nuns are called "Sister" in the West. Aunt Jemima is an American caricature of a self-effacing, very servile woman. I thought of this after sitting in a Boudernath café and hearing the young man who ran the café brag to his friend that his sister was a very experienced senior ani – who was "so high up in the hierarchy," that she was "actually the Rinpoche's personal cook!"
**Quote from Rabbi Hillel.

Bored*

I am as bored as I can be.
There is no tragedy impending.
Just at this moment, the world is not ending.
How can I live without drama?
Today I did my practice and ate my food.
I am in a terrible mood.
Since I feel neither terrified nor forlorn,
It is as if I were never born.
Tonight I'll wash my face and go to bed.
I do not wish that I were dead.
I really must be sick in the head.
Woe is me! There is nothing the matter.

12-28-08

Note

*A little spoof on the American "cult of psychotherapy." Everyone goes to a psychotherapist; if you think there is nothing wrong with you, there must be something terribly wrong with you!

Nisha and Putsky

1.

Nepal Night

A hundred blankets

Cannot warm my frozen, aching bones,

My lonely, aching heart.

Mother and father and aunts and uncles all dead.

I do not know my cousins' last names or their addresses.

When I write to old friends these days, I do not know what to say.

The world we lived in together has become alien to me,

And they do not grasp the reality of my current life.

Today I live among new strangers.

I write to old friends, who have become old strangers.

2.

Nepal Afternoon

A girl and her dog stand in a vacant, littered lot.

Stray cows, stray sheep, stray chickens wander by amidst the rubbish.

The girl and her dog look up as I sit on my roof, and the girl calls out

"Ani-la! Ani-la! Ani-la!" and waves to me.

I wave back. I come down and unlock my gate and let them in,

And we sit on my roof and feast together on Nepalese tangerines and

imported cheese.

The dog gobbles down tangerines as fast as I can peel them.

My young Nepalese friend is lonely too. Her husband is far away,

working in Hong Kong.

Her name is Nisha. Nisha, who is twenty-seven and has long, straight, brown hair down to her waist, tells me I remind her of her mother, and her eyes fill up with tears every time she hugs me.

She visits every day, together with her little black dog named Putsky.

"What is that name again? Please repeat your dog's name" I ask incredulously.

"Putsky," she answers quite clearly. "The name of my dog is Putsky."

This section of Kathmandu where we live is like the Bronx. Its residents are neither cosmopolitan nor sophisticated.

Nisha is not a world traveler. She has never been outside of Nepal,

Nor has she ever met a Russian or a Jew or an American before me,

Yet somehow she decided to name her little black dog "Putsky."

How could this happen?

Surely, it must be magic – a blessing of my only father-guru

That I, who am stranded in this foreign land, alone and with a broken heart

Should manage to meet the only other Russian-Jewish dog in all of Nepal.

It is my delight to share tangerines and cheese each afternoon on my roof with Nisha and Putsky.

3.

Homesick

Will I ever again travel back to the twenty-first century world of indoor heating and the joyful brightness of electric lights turned on at will in the nighttime,

Or ever again lie in a warm bed and look out of my window at a well-lit, well-paved, cleanly swept avenue?

Buses, trains, trolleys, busy people living busy lives will rush by

And I will get caught in the rhythm.

Who were Nisha and Putsky? Only characters in a dream.

I will soon forget the girl and her dog looking up and her waving and calling out to me from a littered lot filled with rubbish, filled with wandering cows, wandering sheep, wandering lonely hearts.

Who were Nisha and Putsky?

I will soon forget them.

I will soon forget them.

I will soon forget them.

But how will I ever forget the beautiful girl with long brown hair and her dog, who eats tangerines?

How will I ever stop seeing her wave and hearing her call out to me?

1-2-09

To Subala

My good friend in Nepal gave me a golden lady Buddha.
She shines on my kitchen table.
My friend Subala tells me I am just like the lady Buddha.
I tell her the Buddha is a reflection of her own mind.

My friend Subala didn't know there were lady Buddhas
Until I told her about them.
My friend Subala didn't believe there were lady Buddhas
Until she looked in the mirror.

1-5-09

Red Cross*

I wish I could put a band aid
On all of the broken places
Where people bleed.
In this make-believe world, where pain feels very real,
Where fear and loneliness is a very big deal,
Suffering, though in the mind, is tangible.
Our suffering defines us.
Our longing for love and wholeness is how we transcend.

There is nothing we can do to fix the situation but practice.**
A band aid cannot adhere to the insubstantial.
Find out the truth and stop spinning your wheels, trying to make
people be different.
There is no one to save or heal.
Still, it is entirely appropriate to offer the heart.

1-9-09

_____

Note

*This is the first poem that was written after leaving the house in
Sukadhara and returning to the UTSE Hotel.
**When dharma teachers or students use the word "practice," this is
always a "shorthand" term for "practice meditation."

Meditation

The hour grows late.

I sit on the roof of my hotel, watching the last contingents of crows head home for supper.

The sky above the mountains hints at pinkness.

My Jasmine tea has grown cold.

My hands have grown cold.

I don't care. I, myself, have become an old crow.

I exist here only in the moment.

I let thoughts about tomorrow fly past as I maintain my seat.

There is one star in the sky. It twinkles directly above my head.

It is a wish-fulfilling star. It shines like the jewel which is my mind.

A poem dictates itself. I light a candle to fulfill this wish of the heart.

Mind writes by the candle's flame as the sky turns dark.

A bird chirps somewhere in the black city.

A driver outside my hotel honks his horn.

I listen to the barking of feral dogs as the candle's flame and my poem both come to an end.

1-13-09

Jewish Renewal Song
(A Letter to Rabbi David)

In the Jewish Renewal Movement, Rabbi David offers the dharma
along with pastrami and eggs,
The path to the end of suffering along with lox and a bagel.
He keeps you very high
Until you die.
Rabbi David helps you to end old destructive habits
By pouring out love and singing the song of a dove
And finding yourself in the characters of the Torah.
He doesn't bore ya
In Jewish Renewal.
Rabbi David explains that you have to get rid of your ego
And see the Oneness of All
By loving your neighbor.
After all, your neighbor is just like you,
Another middle class Jew
Who wants to transcend the trite.
For spiritual freedom he's ready to fight
But gives up nothing.
Rabbi David is full of schmaltz,
(which is Jewish grease).
And here is a plug:
He's always available for a hug.
Then he makes the announcement that you are God.
We are all God.
All you have to do is get rid of your ego.
Then we all go

To heaven together.

The First Noble Truth of Suffering is easily forgotten.

His congregants' ears are stuffed with cotton

When the part of the story about leaving the palace and risking your

welfare and all of your status and giving up all your credentials comes up.

Come on over and sup

On chopped liver and matzoh ball soup.

You don't need to jump through a hoop,

Or even begin at the beginning with every day meditation.

Just declare yourself God,

And in the same breath,

Declare yourself egoless.

And what of the path?

Don't kindle his wrath.

He's a middle class Jew who thinks he is owed enlightenment.

It's his entitlement

For being well-born and educated.

David, it's a lot of vomit.

You have to give up everything.

There is no easy way to pursue the dharma;

You can't just declare yourself God,

Or this holy universe, which exists in a dream, will turn against you.

You will become haunted by the magical forces of your own mind.

I don't mean to be unkind.

Your mind is not a thing;

It is living energy, which is very real.

A candle burning in the darkness gives off light,

But if one is not careful, it consumes the person who ignites it.

• • •

This song was written to Rabbi David by candlelight in the blacked out city of Kathmandu,
Where I presently reside,
Although I do not exist here.
 I decided to search out the sense of the words which we both mimicked so well,
So I traveled to hell,
To a medieval city without sanitation, indoor heating or lights.
My home is a cave.
Although I am not particularly brave,
Karma insisted upon it.
Karma has pushed me forward to do the unthinkable,
And in doing the unthinkable,
I realized that both Self and Other were phony constructs based upon fear.
Only Mind is here.
And fear's attempts to solidify that which is not solid have been undone.

●　●　●

I decided to share this with Rabbi David, although uninvited.
While he might be slighted,
I no longer fear being snickered at for such minor indiscretions.

<u>Note</u>

Sent from Kathmandu, Nepal by Karma Kagyu Lineage Holder Jangchup Peta Paldren Chokyi to Rabbi David Ingber in New York City on 1-14-09. (She was formerly known by that rabbi as Bird Neshama Gelman.)

Burning Garbage

In Kathmandu, they are burning garbage.

The children are striking matches and throwing them on top of the piles of

Rotting waste,

Stinking food,

Stinking snot,

Stinking what-not,

That has been thrown into the streets and gathered at the curbs.

The foul odor rises up to my nostrils,

Even here on the roof where I sit

Watching the sun disappear, under a blue sky decorated with pink and white clouds.

Crows take breaks from flying. They perch everywhere.

The sky above the mountains turns red. Its glow warms me.

Though it is an alien sky, I sit here unafraid.

I have more in common with the crows, who glide gracefully above the mountain tops, across the sky, passing over my head

Than I do with the people of Kathmandu, who burn their rotting waste,

Stinking food,

Stinking snot,

Stinking what-not

Every evening on the streets.

The crows mind their own business, follow their own flight plans, and do not burn garbage in the city, sending up a foul odor into the air.

It is obvious to me who has more sense.

It is obvious to me which is the more intelligent species in Kathmandu.
Who befouls Kathmandu?
Man do!

1-17-09

Haircut

I got a haircut today.
The barber was an artist with scizzors.
He didn't play.
He cut each tiny imperfection away.
Now my head is a shining example
Of what a Karma Kagyu monastic head should look like.
He massaged my scalp.
His hands reached right down into my brain
And stretched each artery and vein
In both of my lobes.
He rubbed my head with his hands.
I became one of his biggest fans.
I will never go to another barber again!

1-17-09

Moban I*

The pigeons gather outside my window.
Their squawking sounds like moaning and groaning,
Moaning and groaning.
They sound agonized. I wish I could relieve their suffering, but I am
helpless.
Their moaning and groaning,
Moaning and groaning
Sounds like it comes from deep inside them,
An expression of pain coming from way down at the bottom of their
guts,
The bottom of their bowels,
A pain that they are impotent to name or find comfort for.
There is nothing wrong. There is no cause for it,
Yet the suffering is endless.

The pigeons moan and groan,
Moan and groan.
They mirror my own agony,
Echoing the sounds I could never stop making
Which rose up in waves from the pit of my stomach into my mouth,
Until my voice could not help give release to them.
This moaning and groaning,
Moaning and groaning
Every night of my life for all of the years that I swallowed Moban
And the moaning and groaning of the pigeons sounds identical to
me.
I am as unable to release those pigeons from their suffering now

As I was unable to help myself then,
Unable to stop my endless, compulsive pain.

1-19-09

Note

*This is a so-called "anti-psychotic" drug that used to be prescribed frequently in the United States. It is prescribed less often these days because of the possible negative side effects.

Moban II

Will I stop convulsing in time to go to work and look normal,
Or will this medicine, prescribed to help me, help me lose my job
because I look so strange?
Because I cannot erase what looks like a snicker from my face?
Because I cannot erase what looks like a scowl, put there by the
muscles in my forehead, which do not stop contracting?
My boss greets me, "Good morning. How are you today?" and I try
in vain to smile at him,
Though my lips are pressed together tightly, held still in one
immutable spot by the medicine.
I just want to stay home with the blanket over my head.
I just want to play dead,
So no one sees me contorted by the Moban.

The Moban stops my mind from flowing freely, my thoughts from
unwinding.
It keeps me safe from my heart. It protects me from my future.
My mind becomes as stiff as my lips, with its artificial snicker.
My mind does not change.
I am temporarily kept safe from impermanence.
I am held safe from my life,
Until a doctor changes my prescription.
Once I stop swallowing Moban, my mind begins its wild and
beautiful dance.
It is resuscitated, and my life comes back to life.
I reel from the sharp stings of so-called "insanity,"
Yet it is so much better than being anesthetized by Moban.
Now I ride the galloping, bucking bronco of karma.

1-20-09

Exile

Kathmandu is surrounded by tall mountains. Every late afternoon, the sky fills up with groups of black crows, headed homeward. Though a mist covers the mountain tops, I can still see a few white snow peaks from the roof of the UTSE Hotel. The crows fly in their direction, though not precisely. As the sun descends behind them, disappearing into some magical resting place, the sky turns rose colored. I stand alone, watching the sky above me turn red as the sun and the crows both return to their homes. When the air grows too chilly for me to remain on the roof, I grope my way downstairs in the darkened hallway to my room on the first floor. There, in the black space, I feel for the candle and the book of matches which I keep on my desk. I place the candle in the holder, which the owner of the hotel has given to me, and I light it. The candle brightens the area around my desk, allowing me to write in the cold darkness. There is no indoor heating in Kathmandu. Though a bright sun warms the daytime sky, the nighttimes are freezing. The owner of the UTSE offers hot water bags to all of the guests. I thank her for her generosity, but refuse to take one. The heat only lasts such a short time, and it is a drop in the bucket. The cold is too pervasive. If there were electricity, the light bulbs would warm up the rooms, but there is none.

When my creative energy has been spent, I move my seat from the chair by my desk to my bed. I am too cold to get undressed and put on my nightgown, so I just unbuckle my bra and slip it out of my sleeve. I should extinguish the candle before lying down, but I do not. I have an insatiable craving for light in my room. I lie down, pulling the quilt and a second blanket over me. I pull the quilt over my head. Though it blocks out most of the light, I know that the candle is still lit. It is knowing that the light is there, the idea of it, which actually matters, much more than the light itself. However, when my pain has reached the critical point, I no longer desire even that. I sit up and blow out the candle.

Now there is nothing left. There is no hope at all.

1-20-09

Nervous Knees

I have nervous knees.

My knees always want to dance, even when there is no music.

They want to run and play,

Even when there are no companions to play with.

My nervous knees keep me awake at night when I want to sleep.

My knees force me to sit upright on the edge of my bed,

Dangling them, when the rest of me wants to lie flat.

The doctors tell me I have restless leg syndrome,

And that there is medicine which will force my knees to keep still.

The only side effects are extreme sexual urges and the desire to gamble.

I may leave my bed to go downstairs and rape my doorman,

But, alas, while my pelvis is busy, my knees will rest.

I'll keep the nervous knees, please.

I don't want to have sex with my doorman,

Or throw all of my rent money into a slot machine.

I prefer to stay up all night and write

While my knees dance a jig underneath my desk,

Rather than swallow a pill and have an orgy with the night staff in my lobby.

I don't want to swallow a pill and gamble

On accruing a much worse life,

By throwing all of my rent money on a lucky number

And finding myself with nowhere to live and no bed for my knees to bounce around on.

Thus, I say no to my kind physician's offer to write me a prescription

And accept my karma as it is, without the intervention of modern, Western science.

1-21-09

A True Revolutionary*

"It could be our karma to rebel against karma, couldn't it?" the
student asked her master.
"Then the rebellion would not really be a rebellion at all," her master
answered.
"I fought against fate my whole life," the student recalled.
"Did you win?" her master asked.
"It was my karma to do so," she answered with a tremor in her voice
that could be taken either for a laugh or the early stage of sobbing.
"I took my whole life to be real," she said.
"It was that confusion which caused me to struggle.
 If I had realized early on that it was a dream, I might have slept
through it all."
"So that ignorance was really intelligence," her master answered.
"And the statement 'Nothing really matters' can be taken two
different ways."
Because Nothing really matters, I am here with you today.
Because Nothing really matters, I light a candle instead of sit in the dark.
Because Nothing really matters, I offer a gift of dharma.
That gift is my life which, although it never took place,
I have lived with the rage and passion of a true revolutionary.

1-21-09

Note

*This poem was written the day after my meeting with His Eminence
Jamgon Kongtrul, Rinpoche, an important tulku in the Karma Kagyu
Lineage of Tibetan Buddhism, and was forwarded to him as part of a
note thanking him for the interview.

Manipulation

My food was full of pepper.
It would have been delicious with just a little garlic or salt.
It would have been so much better had they just served it plain.
I desired a good meal, but I wished for it in vain.
Still, I could almost taste the food's goodness underneath all of the
pepper.
My face was covered with powder.
I put blue lines on top of my eyelids and red paint all over my lips
Because I wanted to be a beauty,
Since I believed that was my duty,
So only a few intimate friends saw my true, friendly face.
My personality was smeared with grease,
So I tried to butter up everyone
And tap dance my way though life,
But I could never seem to learn all of the steps well enough.
The world said "Tough!"
And no one was particularly kind.
If they had been, I might have stayed blind
And continued stumbling all over my own feet.

It was when I stopped dancing and just sat down,
That I stopped playing the role of a clown.
It was when I looked in the mirror of my mind,
That I finally stopped being blind
To all of the beauty and magic I tried to crank up artificially
Which were mine by nature.

When I leave off wearing my watch to the meditation hall

And simply allow myself to be there,

My practice becomes easier and I do not get a backache.

When I stop trying to fix my thoughts and quit declaring war on my mind,

But allow it to be as it is,

It stops being my enemy and my life becomes more pleasant.

1-24-09

Faber's Fascination:*
An Overeaters' Meditation Song**

Whenever I look up at the sky,
I start to ask myself, "Who am I?"
So I run to buy a pizza pie.
Om mani peme hum.
Om mani peme hum.
Whenever I look up at the moon,
My heart starts to sing a melancholy tune,
So I run indoors and grab my spoon.
Om mani peme hum.
Om mani peme hum.
Whenever I see a baby pup
And look into his eyes and then pick him up,
I want to eat a second sup.
Om mani peme hum.
Om mani peme hum.
Whenever I feel much tenderness,
I accuse myself of being a mess,
And turn right away to the garlic press.
Om mani peme hum.
Om mani peme hum.
Whenever I must dine alone,
I always eat a second scone.
Instead, why not try writing a poem?
Om mani peme hum.
Om mani peme hum.
Oh, why not try to just sit with your mind,
And admit to yourself that you are not blind,
To all of the love and pain in your heart?

Om mani peme hum.

Om mani peme hum.

A pizza pie will just make you so heavy,

You may feel like you want to jump into the levee.

And if you continue to beat up your brain,

That will only cause it to rain.

If you run away to the pastry shop,

That will not make your feelings stop.

If you try to drink or smoke them away,

You may not last for many a day.

The only solution that can work,

Is to realize that you are no jerk,

And that your own heart is the Ultimate Goal.

There is no authority at some opposite pole,

Who has got all the answers and everything right.

All this self-deprecation is the cause of your plight.

When we sit with our minds, then we tear down the wall,

Which is up in order to cover it all,

To pretend that we are other than Heart,

From intense emotions separate and apart.

We are just Mind. Our feelings are Wisdom.

We don't need to fight them or make them be different.

It is perfectly perfect just to be who we are.

(Hands in or out of the cookie jar).

Om mani peme hum.

Om mani peme hum.

1-25-09

_____

Notes

*Faber's Fascination – I lived with my parents in Coney Island,
Brooklyn from the age of 12 to the age of 20. Immediately across

the street from the Coney Island subway station at Stillwell Avenue, there was an amusement park ride called Faber's Fascination. I had to stand staring at that sign, sometimes for an hour or more, each time I got out of the subway and waited for the bus to my home. Years later, after I began practicing the dharma, I remembered that sign and decided it was a label or an instruction for understanding samsara; we are held in samsara by a kind of fascination. In reality, there is nothing to it. Samsara is like an amusement park ride in the sense that we become worked up by it, like we get worked up on a roller coaster ride, but in reality, it is insubstantial and impermanent.
**Overeaters – For my last five years in New York, I was a member of two Anonymous programs: Nicotine Anonymous and Overeaters Anonymous. These two programs are based on the original Alcoholics Anonymous program and follow the same twelve steps. My membership in these programs was extremely helpful and changed my life for the better.

Two

I have two of everything on my desk:
Two bottles of water,
Two candles,
Two boxes of matches,
Two pens,
Two chocolate cookies,
Two golden images of Buddha.
In my bathroom, I have two towels,
Two roles of toilet paper,
Two packets of dental floss,
And two bars of soap.
My hotel room contains two beds.
It has two lamps – one next to each bed.
When I want to go out,
I have two coats and two pairs of shoes to choose from.
When I want to stay in,
I can choose from two books to read
Or two malas* to practice my meditation with.

If there were not two,
There would be none.
Since everything is relative,
There is no such thing as one.
If you do not exist,
Neither do I.
When I think I love you,
That is the reason why.

When I think I hate you,
That is the reason too.
There would be no such thing as a gentile,
If there were no Jew.
There would be no such thing as a Buddha,
Unless someone behaved like a fool.
If there were nothing to manipulate,
There would be no such thing as a tool.
If there were no candle,
No one would light a match.
If nobody pitched,
Then no one would catch.
If I never felt sadness,
I would never feel joy.
If there were no children,
Who would ever invent a toy?
If no person were black,
No person would be white.
If there were no armies,
No nations would fight.
Thus the whole universe
That comes into being
Is like an illusion
That I am seeing.
I see the whole world,
Without any real eye.
It is all seen,
Without any I.

The dance of all things
Is the dance of zero.
If you think they exist,
Then your mind is your Pharaoh.
If you would like
To cross the Red Sea,
You are welcome to come along,
And practice meditation with me.

1-26-09

Note

*A string of Buddhist prayer or meditation beads. There are always 109 beads on a mala. It is helpful to use a mala when doing certain repetitive practices which require that one keeps count.

Uncle Irving

My Uncle Irving was a very kind man to me.
His family was of a superior pedigree,
And although he did not have a law degree,
He washed his face every day.
He always brought me a gift
In order to give me a lift.
A bottle of cheap drugstore cologne,
That was full of bologne,
And came with the unwritten message, "Fuck you" pasted to the
bottle.
Cousin Carol was very superior,
Always reminding me I was inferior
Because I wore her hand-me down dresses and old shoes.
I had the blues,
So to compete with my mind I did choose,
And studied and studied and studied to make things be different.

But no matter how hard I tried,
In the end, for their help I cried,
Because somehow, things always turned out shitty
And Irving and Carol, with eyes full of pity,
Treated me with so much arrogant kindness,
It turned my guts inside out.
Uncle Irving told me I was a weak person,
And I believed him, so I turned to self-cursin'.
Every time I saw him, I was filled with shame
Because of self-blame.

In this nightmare, when I was fourteen,

Irving smiled and was not mean,

And whispered into my ear,

 "You make me feel things for you that I am not supposed to feel."

I was horrified by my appeal

And ran away from him.

The situation was grim.

I thought, "This is what I deserve for being such a low class girl."

Irving always felt pity for me

For being my bum father's daughter.

I also bought her –

That image of a self which had no reality whatsoever.

The karma of believing in that lie became a life.

It became a world. It became birth and death.

And though no one was really here,

We shed many a tear,

That is, both the self and the world, which were naught but mind's
illusions.

Many years later, when Irving got cancer,

He thought that being strong was the answer,

Taking care of himself and not asking for help.

"Do not yelp" he ordered himself, "in spite of the pain."

His attempt was in vain.

When the pain did peak,

And the compassion of others he needed to seek,

He called himself weak

And committed suicide by stuffing his head into a plastic bag.

"Uncle Irving is dead," mother said.

"You should come to the funeral."

But being no saint,
(A phony picture I will not paint),
Not only did I avoid the funeral,
But also celebrated the manner in which he died.

1-27-09

Long Division

You be this,
And I'll be that.
You wear the coat,
And I'll wear the hat.
You can be Joan.
I'll call myself Pat.
What do you know? It's the world!
Imagine that!
You can be white,
And I'll be brown.
You wear the pants.
I'll wear the gown.
Every time you smile,
I will cry and frown.
What do you know? It's the world!
Imagine that!
You be the master.
I'll be the slave.
You can be smart.
I'll be a knave.
You can call me a coward,
But I will still call you brave.
What do you know? It's the world!
Imagine that!
You can drink water.
I will drink beer.
In the end, it's all the same, my dear.

Neither one of us is really here,

Yet at the same time, we are positively real.

1-28-09

Intentions*

Today I had good intentions,
But somehow things turned out bad.
I was fully determined to be happy,
But instead, I wound up sad.
I wanted to write an article,
But ended up writing a poem.
I wanted a piece of chocolate cake,
But ended up eating a scone.
I wanted to study the dharma,
Instead I caught up on my French.
I wanted to sit home on my sofa,
But found myself on a park bench.
I was hoping to eat soup for dinner,
But instead, I settled for rice.
I wanted to rent a bungalow,
But found it infested with mice.
I intended to go to the movies,
But ended up at a dance.
I had hoped to buy a villa in Spain,
But bought one in the South of France.
I ordered coffee on my coffee break;
Instead, I was served tea.
So I wonder what is going on here.
Is there something the matter with me?
Is everyone's mind inside out and backwards,
Or am I the one that's the fool?
Why do I have such a hard time with life,

When I always got A in school?
Is the problem that I am too smart,
Or is it that I am too dumb?
When I come to you wearing my Sunday best,
You make me feel like a bum.
When I come to you with a heart full of love,
You send me home with a bitter tongue.
I want to see you mounting a throne,
You want to see me hung.
I offer you a golden chalice,
You present me with a suicide knife.
So I guess there is nothing more I can do,
Than simply accept my life.
Since you have taken away the sugar,
I always crave something sweet.
Since you have removed all my supports,
I must stand on my own two feet.

1-30-09

Note

*After I completed this poem, I realized it was addressed to my root guru and the Vajradhatu-Shambhala community which he created. The ruthless compassion of the vajrayana path forces one to grow up, unlike the phony kindness of the samsaric world, which keeps one wrapped in the cocoon of perpetual childhood, very cozy and safe from life.

Blind Pain

I do not experience blind pain today.

I sit at the window in my hotel, looking out at Shanghai Fast Food and the Tibetan Guest House.

The popcorn and peanut lady strolls by with her cart.

Whatever happens, it is all in a day's work.

The MS Omer Art Emporium floods the street with music.

The cadences in the singer's voice make her sound like a cantor in a Brooklyn synagogue.

I drink a cup of black tea for breakfast. I accept that it is not coffee.

Just for today, I swallow the black liquid without choking on it.

I do not experience blind pain today.

I relax on Jyatha in Thamel, Kathmandu. In the illusion which I call my life, this is where I live now.

Just for the moment, one illusion is as good as the next. One fantasy of a city street is as good as any other.

Maybe in the future, I will attend the Metropolitan Opera at Lincoln Center in New York City once again.

Maybe I will see the ballet "Swan Lake" performed one more time before I die

And maybe not.

I do not experience blind pain today.

1-31-09

Aunt Acid*

I took a walk through the market today
In order to walk my panic away
And buy a new yellow shirt.
All the shirts that I saw were purple and blue.
Of yellow, they only had a few
Which were much too small to fit me.
I stopped and bought a Nepalese cake
To try something different and my true feelings fake
And pretend to myself that I don't detest everything Nepalese.
"This cake is delicious" I told myself,
Behaving like a mental elf
By trying to feel and think what I thought I should.
Later that night, I threw the cake away.
That behavior belonged to a former day –
Trying to be what everyone, especially myself, tells me I am supposed to.

"You should love other cultures"
(Though the people are vultures).
"All men are brothers"
(They just behave like a bunch of mothers).
"You should always forgive"
(Let the murderer-rapist-arsonist live
To rape and kill again).
And above all, always vote Democratic.
(FDR was god in the flesh).
But with my experience, this doesn't mesh.

All of these simple axioms for how to live and be in the world just
don't work for me anymore.
You should love all the poor
Just because they are poor
Has grown old in my mind, has become dated, and is a bore.
The only thing I can do today
Is to let go of all preconceptions about how to be,
Allow the energy of love and hate and joy and pain to flow free.
Since there is no me,
(For I am only a beautiful ghost who exists in a dream),
There is no need to grasp on to principles which sound lofty but are
untrue,
Which people take to be holy writ, but in practice, only increase
suffering.
Today I would prefer the hard search for truth instead of fancy lies,
Earning joyful enlightenment after the long practice of patience.

2-1-09

Note:

*If I am going to be called an aunt, at least I'll be Aunt Acid rather
than Aunt Jemina!

Chinese Bread

I went to Shanghai Fast Food last night
To order some Chinese bread.
I tried to describe what I wanted,
But the waiter could not understand what I said.
Two Tibetan monks were sitting nearby
And heard me struggling with words.
They listened as they sipped their chicken soup
And swallowed their rice with curds.
"What are you trying to order, Ani?"
They asked, but they did so in vain,
Since I did my best to ignore them
Because their presence created too much pain.
I sat down, and they looked at me and smiled
And asked in good English, "Where are you from?"
"New York!" I could not avoid answering through clenched teeth
And scowled at them and looked glum.
Then right away, I turned my back
Which ended the conversation.
This behavior did not bring me any joy,
And I am sure it caused them no elation.
The monks just wanted to be sociable and kind,
And I am so lonely and far from all my friends.
When I see such monks, I want to reach out with love,
Yet with rage and pain it ends.
Once I got my food, I crossed the street to my hotel
And went back to my room and cried.
I cannot accept being a well-treated inferior.
Though I love you, I have vajra pride.
If you tell me that I may not stand shoulder-to-shoulder with you as
an equal,

And you expect me to stand back with a lowered head,
Then you are turning my love against me, to choke on it.
Vomiting fake kindness and leaving me for dead.
It is not okay to be an owner of slaves
And say, "But I feed them a tasty dinner."
Unless every person who so chooses may run in a race,
Whoever wins is a phony winner.

"You monks, I hope you choke on your dinner.
You may keep your hypocritical kindness."
I think this, yet to pretend my heart is not filled with tears
As it hears my mind's words would be blindness.*
Because I will not allow you to turn my love against me,**
I may not be beloved by you.
Still, I will not collaborate in pretending to be an adjunct monastic.
I deserve the same rights and status as you.
One day soon, a little girl Karmapa tulku*** will be discovered,
And she will sit on the vajra throne.****
She will perform the Black Hat ceremony*****
And the title "Dharma Queen" own.******

Since it created the trigger to write this,
It was worth choking on the Chinese bread.
And if it ignites the karma which fulfills this prediction,
It was worth the pain in my head.

2-1-09

Notes

*This situation of inequality between monks and nuns reminds me of
a scene in the movie "Yentl" about the Orthodox Jews who lived in
the shtetls (ghettos) of Czarist Russia. Yentl accompanied her father

to synagogue, but she was forced to sit separately upstairs in a balcony because she was a woman. When he fell down on the floor with a heart attack, she was thus unable to reach him in time to help. This type of situation evokes an awful combination of love and rage at once.

 **Turn my love against me – In other words, I will not say because I love my lineage or my sangha, I will allow myself to be made into a second class citizen. If I am told that I should step back as a token of love, this is incorrect. It is love's duty to step forward, not back.
***A tulku is a reincarnated great teacher. The Karmapa tulku is the head of the Karma Kagyu lineage. Thus far, the Karmapa tulku has always been a man. ****Karmapa's throne, indestructible throne.
*****The ceremony of the Black Crown may only be performed by His Holiness Karmapa. This ceremony is extremely special in that it guarantees enlightenment in a single lifetime to anyone who has the good fortune to witness it. I had this good fortune when I first joined Vajradhatu, many years ago in San Francisco. The former Karmapa, Ranjung Rigpe Dorje, visited that city very shortly after I became a member. Although I was brand new and had no status or credentials whatsoever, somehow I managed to get a seat which provided me with a perfect view of the entire ceremony.
******Past and current Karmapas have been referred to as Dharma Kings.

Gaia's

I have found some respite in the hell realm ---
A very fine restaurant.
The waiters aren't idiots –
They don't stand at my table and grunt.
They have managed to ensure adequate lighting,
Which in Kathmandu is very exciting.
They open promptly at 7:00 every day,
So I don't have to stand outside mornings and pray.
They play soft classical music in the background.
Of the usual throat clearing and spitting, I do not hear a sound.
Their coffee is excellent (almost on par with French roast).
Of this restaurant named Gaia's, I have to boast.
Everyone is polite and the atmosphere is relaxing,
So that eating a meal there is joyful rather than taxing,
And you may sit as long as you like
Without the manager suggesting that you take a hike.
The food is healthful, tasty and inexpensive.
If you want my recommendation, I won't have to grow pensive.
If you ever have the misfortune to be in Kathmandu,
I recommend Gaia's restaurant to you.
(It is just off Jyatha in Thamel.)
It is like a tiny heaven in the midst of hell.

2-2-09

Not Practicing

This morning, I went to the bank machine.
There was no money in my account.
I wanted to look for work on the Internet,
But the electric power was out.
I had decided to save money to return to New York,
But karma forced me to spend it.
I try to wipe the terror out of my mind:
In what ghastly way will karma end it?
One moment I am feeling confident,
The next, sick with fear beyond belief.
Even when I have money to pay my bills,
I worry about a thief.
I know that no matter what I think or do,
If my karma is that I'm to be destroyed,
Then that will be the end of my life,
No matter how much good sense I've employed.

For all the fine words we say to ourselves
To explain the world are untrue.
Our thoughts and beliefs have nothing at all
To do with what we actually do.
And everything we experience
Is a karmically produced illusion.
Though I would prefer to think in a positive way,
I cannot avoid this conclusion.
My guru is my karma externalized,
And he is my own True Heart.

Thus I try to have faith in Basic Goodness,
To avoid falling apart.
Still, it is difficult to maintain equilibrium
When the ground underneath me shakes.
I cannot pretend blindness by waving a flag,
In front of my eyes
To notice nothing
As my whole world breaks.

Just for today, I have enough money to pay last month's bills
And not a penny more.
This morning, I was feeling confident.
At this moment, I feel frightened and poor.
And I cannot avoid asking the question,
Will the guru grind me into the dust?
Will karma leave me sitting helpless in isolation and terror
Here in Nepal until I bust?
Will the Karma Kagyu guru turn me into the street
To beg in a foreign land?
To be homeless and die of hunger and thirst,
Crawling in the sand?
This dharma is life. It is not a practice.
It is neither a game nor a religion.
I thought I was playing with something other than truth,
Pecking at crumbs, like a pigeon.**

But when I looked into my life and my mind,
I found myself in a cage.***
Now my mind is a mixture of hope and fear,
Shock, self-compassion and outrage.

At this moment, the guru's blessing feels more like a curse.
Will things get better or will things get worse?
At least, since I am inseparable from him,
I can behave gently toward myself to avoid getting even more
grim.***

2-2-09

Notes

*and **When students first come to practice "the Buddhist religion,"
it is a very part time practice to them, separate from the rest of their
lives. Thus, they are pecking at crumbs. Over time, one finds there is
no separation between the dharma and life. Dharma is life itself; not
one isolated portion of it called "religion." One comes to understand
that one's life situation is choiceless; there is no escape from Mind;
thus one is in a cage. There is never the choice of "not practicing
today" unless one also chooses to "not breathe today."
***Since I am inseparable from the guru, whenever I am feeling
terrible, I always ask myself, "How would I treat him (the character
Mr. Mukpo, i.e. Chogyam Trungpa, in his 'separate, physical form')
if he were in this situation?" Because I love him so much, the answer
is inevitably "with utter gentleness" or "with the most tender, loving
care in order to make sure, to the best of my ability, that he survives
and remains well." Thus, I must treat myself in that same way.
Therefore, it could be said that the same love or devotion which got
me into all of this (challenging practice) is also my saving grace. I
feel certain I would not be alive today were it not for loving the guru
(devotion).

The Motley Modules*

My coffee was full of grease today.
There were a million motley modules of muck
Floating at the top of my cup.
I told the waiter to take it away.
"I would like to drink a clean cup of coffee, if I may."
However, there was nothing more I could think of to say,
When he replaced the million motley modules of muck
With a meager ten million more.
At first, I was tempted to get sore.
But having recently committed myself to practicing the paramita of
patience,**
I let a friendly fly drink from the rim of the cup
And settled for a spot of tea with my sup.
This turned out to be a delightful change
Which I didn't arrange,
But arose spontaneously as a kind of karma as nonlethal as the motley
modules probably would have been.

2-2-09

Note

*This poem is an example of the gentle, loving care mentioned in the previous poem, "Not Practicing." When I wrote the previous poem, I was sick with terror. One way I dealt with it was by writing this little, funny, frivolous one to divert my focus away from the extreme anxiety. "The Motley Modules" proved effective!

**A paramita is a transcendent virtue. The paramita of patience
is transcendent patience. There are six paramitas to be practiced
by bodhisattvas ("buddhas-in-training") in Mahayana Buddhism:
discipline, generosity, patience, effort, meditation and wisdom.

Maitri is Running Low on Sap Today*

Maitri is running low on sap today.
I cannot do those things I usually do here.
Maitri is running low on sap today.
It has all been drained by loneliness and terror.
I do not want to sit and type my poems.
I do not want to go to the café and eat ice cream.
Today I will not hunt for the grape vendor.
I will not browse the market place.
I will remain in my room.
Maitri is running low on sap,
For I am nowhere on the map
Close to where I would like to be,
And I am haunted by the awful fear
That I will never get from here to there,
And that I will die in Kathmandu
Penniless and alone.

2-2-09

Note

*Maitri is pronounced like "my tree." This is a Buddhist term for
loving kindness towards oneself and one's own mind. Notice the date
it was written is the same as the previous two poems. One way I dealt
with the fearful feelings was to "share about them" by writing. Even
if no human heard me, I knew that Ms. Pen and Mr. Paper heard me.
Ms. Pen and Mr. Paper are the oldest friends I have. We have been
best friends ever since I met them in the first grade. Allowing myself

to share with them when I was feeling so badly is a perfect example of the tender, loving care I wrote about earlier. Since I am a Trungpa tulku, maitri and my love for my guru (devotion) are one and the same.

Toilet Bowl

This whole world is tinsel and crud from top to bottom.

Anything of value gets thrown into a ditch and shit on.

In this karmic nightmare of a life, I pass through the world expecting no esteem at all.

All the esteem is reserved for fools and charlatans.

Why would my practice or my art be considered of value here in this world, which is nothing other than samsara's toilet bowl?

2-4-09

Ghost

This afternoon, I sit in Gaia's restaurant, surrounded by Europeans.
Their pale faces, and the sounds of their familiar languages are
comforting.
I can pretend to be at home. I can pretend that I was ever at home at
home.
I can pretend that I was not born an alien, and have not been an alien
everywhere my entire life.

I try to fit in,
To change this or that, rearrange this or that, study the ways of the
world and make it better.
I march on picket lines. I sit down at sit-ins. I lie down at lie-ins.
As a teenager, I spend my weekdays in school and my weekends in the
Women's House of Detention.
Things change just enough for me to share a victory toast
And then go home alone after the cheering has ended.*

I am a ghost on retreat
Because I was born a ghost on retreat.
My guru did not create the situation
But only served to clarify it.
Now my heart friends of the past inform me that I have become more
gentle and loving.
Though I am not really here, I thank them for whatever positive
attributions they affectionately bestow upon me.

112

I send them my love and carry their love with me as I move forward as a ghost along my secret path.

2-5-09

Note

*I was very active in the American civil rights movement of the 1960's. Often after a demonstration or after being released from jail, the group of demonstrators went back to headquarters to celebrate.

Courage

Hey ho! Sho mo!
My life has become an outrageous adventure.
I cannot wait to discover what will happen in the next moment.
I cannot bear to image in what will happen next.
Emptiness haunts me; it follows me everywhere, biting at my ankles
as I walk.
Either I whirl into a panic or do a dance of delight.
Though in my mind's darkest spaces, it is always fright and fight,
Still, I can battle the terror more courageously in the sunlight.
Next week, I am going to India, like my father Marpa*, who never
existed.
I will live beside the mountains, which will either lend me strength or
terrorize me or both.
I have given up clinging to the notion of that self who lived in the past.
Since the dharma is vast
And is nothing other than my life,
I am able to stop shaking and come out from under the bed,
At least for the present moment.

2-5-09

Note

Marpa was a great yogin and founding parent of the Karma Kagyu
Lineage.

Renunciation
(A Reformed Overeater's Song)

When I am so lonely I could die,
I can't replace love with an apple pie.
It will sicken me to eat and cry.
Om mani peme hum. Om mani peme hum.
I have so much sadness in my heart,
There is no kind of food which will make it depart.
My life is too sour; my world is too tart.
Om mani peme hum. Om mani peme hum.
I want to reach out to a human being,
Even if she's just an illusion I'm seeing,
This constant nightmare of loneliness freeing,
Om mani peme hum. Om mani peme hum.
I want to tell someone how I feel,
Compared to a sangha, food has no appeal,
So I will throw away that extra meal,
Om mani peme hum. Om mani peme hum.

I can't bear to sit here all alone,
And stuff my mouth with an ice cream cone
When I really want to call a friend on the phone.
Om mani peme hum. Om mani peme hum.
So I'll throw that kilo of grapes in the trash,
And get rid of all that lousy hash.
To say I need others doesn't abash.
Om mani peme hum. Om mani peme hum.
Cause food doesn't give me what I need.

It just makes me ill to feed and feed.
To compulsive overeating, I wish godspeed.
Om mani peme hum.
Om mani peme hum.

2-6-09

Megan*
(The Bellydancer)

The outrageous energy of untamed sexuality
She trained and disciplined.
She rode the horse unbridled, yet dominated it.
She was a beautiful human animal
Displaying her myriad vivid colors with agility.

She was the best of me,
She was the worst of me.
She was the wisest of me,
She was the stupidest.
She was the mirror of my heart,
She was the mirror of my mind.
She was my anger and my cruelty,
She was me, gentle and kind.
She was me at the age of fourteen,
Dancing for the neighborhood boys,
Begging to be loved,
Giving away all of my toys.
She was me with her face in the mirror
Agonizing over each new line,
Thinking that beauty was something else
More youthful and more divine.
She was me, giving myself lessons
In everything my heart already knew
But could not accept until she said the words,
Back in those days when I beat myself black and blue.

How to nurture myself and be my own kind mother,
Feeding the inner child with love so that she could grow,
How to soothe the beautiful, wild horse of mind
When she went into a frenzy, spinning wild,
Over the word "No."

She was me, licking the poison of self-hatred,
For being battered by senseless fools,
Devastated for not winning the idiot prize
Awarded by lizards, monkeys and mules.
She was me, with the notion there were others to be jealous of,
Not realizing she was All,
Churning her guts inside out,
Though she was beautiful, elegant and tall.
She was me, reminding myself to keep the faith of the heart
Because we are magical beings in a magical realm
In which pain and love dance together as heavenly partners
With Truth pounding out rhythm at the helm.
That Truth is that we are all beyond meeting and parting.
There are no lizards, monkeys or mules outside of one's own mind.**
Our life is a path of twists and turns,
And at the end, what do we find?
This poem will have to end with a cliff-hanger
Since I don't want to just mimic concepts which seem correct
So I will have to take further steps
Along my journey, my heart's truth to inspect.
For there are no answers outside of myself,
No happiness to come from any other.
With gentle humility, I offer this poem to Megan the bellydancer,
My best friend, my sister, my daughter and my mother.

She whose magical dance gives birth to life and joy,
Expresses in movement what I do my best to express in words.
Both are ways to uplift the spirit,
So that we soar through the sky like birds.

2-8-09

_____

Note

*Megan was my sponsor for a little over a year in the 12 Step Program, Overeaters Anonymous. Our work together during that year turned my life entirely around. We have been friends ever since. **Neither are there any great gurus outside of one's mind. As Trungpa, Rinpoche told me in response to a compliment I gave him, "Look into your own mind." Your mind is the home of the guru. It is the place which gives birth to all and in which all reside. There is no other place.

Kak

Tonight I sit on the roof of the UTSE Hotel
Enjoying the cool air and a half kilo of green grapes with my black
crow friends.
I have climbed up here to celebrate my imminent departure for India,
To have a going away party in which the crows and I share sweet
fruit.

I put a grape down on the table next to where I am sitting.
A crow swoops down and grabs it with his long beak.
I put down another and another. I eat another and another.
One for the crow. One for me. One for him. One for me.
This is how we party.

It is wonderful to have made so many good friends in Nepal.
Hundreds of crows fill the sky above me, flapping their wings and
crying "Kak! Kak! Kak!"
"Kak" is crow language for good-bye. Good luck in Dharmasala."
"Kak" is also their idiomatic expression meaning "We will miss you."

I will miss the crows I met in Kathmandu
Who flew from Tibet over the mountain tops and across the skies
above the UTSE Hotel on their way to India.
Maybe I will meet some of them again in Dharmasala,
Though it may be difficult to discern old friends from new.
Some people might say, "You've seen one crow, you've seen them all"
with a casual shrug of the shoulders,
But from my vantage point as a bird, I know better than that

And can state unequivocally that each crow is a very special individual and deserves his own green grape, at the very least.

2-10-09

Part Three:
Welcome to India - 2/12/09
through 4/11/09

Fruition

I stand on my terrace in McLeod Ganj at nightfall
Surrounded by mountains and tall trees.
In the distance is the white peak of a snow mountain.
I am certain it is Lachi Snow Mountain.
I am certain it is Milarepa's snow mountain.
I have found the home of my heart.
From the woods, I hear the chatter of little animals.
It is wonderful to be surrounded by such good friends.
The Tibetan tea here is so delicious, I have forgotten all about coffee.
The stars are so bright, I have forgotten city lights.
In Nepal, I cried and prayed to go home day and night.
Here in India, there is nothing more to pray for.

2-16-09

Breakfast

Hey ho!

There is nothing more delicious than a big bowl of thogkpa*, a hard
boiled egg, and Tibetan tea for breakfast.

There is nothing more wonderful than sitting and looking out at
Lachi Snow Mountain while eating breakfast.

A hearty meal is good.

A hearty life is good.

Why suffer needlessly?

Little girl, about five years old, an adorable human flower,

Is tiny Tibetan ballerina.

I teach her English by lifting a noodle out of my bowl and repeating

"Noodle Noodle Noodle" while dangling it in the air.

Tiny Tibetan girl and grown American ani both love noodles.

We love oodles of noodles,

Oodles of noodles for breakfast.

2-17-09

Notes

*Tibetan noodle soup, eaten as a staple.

Meeting Karmapa

I met His Holiness Karmapa today.
I met His Holiness Karmapa today,
So I keep telling myself. So I keep repeating.
So I keep trying to brainwash my brain.
I saw the form of His Holiness Karmapa today,
A tall young man, dressed in red and yellow, standing in the center of
a large hall,
Handing out red strings to the people who filed past him.
Red strings
Protection for the mind brings.
And people of faith and people of less faith who were on holiday
came to get them and be blessed by him.
For some, it was like going to the theatre or to a circus,
But for others, it was an act of faith which required some sacrifice.
The young man called Karmapa stood handing out strings –
Strings which protection for meditator's mind brings.
His face was expressionless. It was totally blank.
He showed no love.
He showed no hate.
All that he did was proper. There was nothing more.
I had hoped to find a warmly purring cat, but there was no warmth
in him.
I had hoped to find eyes that laughed, a spirit that danced, but he was
not so adorned.
"Just for today," I thought, "emptiness remains vacant. The door of
Karmapa is open, but no one is at home."
I left the form of Karmapa feeling angry and disappointed.

"Emptiness has not given birth to joy," I said to myself.

Still, when I saw the white snow mountains, I began singing,

And when I sat down with my friend at home, he answered the exact question I had gone to Karmapa to ask

And then transmitted the exact empowerment I had gone to seek.

He did both of these things without me asking him anything or telling him anything at all.

He is a new friend who barely knows me and is not Kagyupa, although he has a very kind heart.

Today I saw the form of His Holiness Karmapa.

Who is this lord anyway? Is there really anything special about the man?

Form is form. There was not much there. He seemed to be simply okay, which was okay.

Form is emptiness. Emptiness is much more than okay.

It is richly full.

Emptiness is pregnant and holy.

If I practice and see Other, I see Karmapa filling the whole world,

But if I practice and win complete enlightenment, do I see the world filled entirely with Karmama?

There is nothing in the world to be seen other than Karma

In its myriad manifestations – Karmapa and Karmama both.

Since they are identical in essence,

It is foolish and pointless to discriminate.*

I see Karmama fly through the sky in the form of a bird.

And climb up the tree in the back of my house in the form of a monkey.

I see Karmama wagging her tail in the form of a dog.

She dresses up in my clothing daily.

I am thus bound to pay tribute to myself,

And live a life that matters, deserving of the highest honor,
As well as honoring all others.

The Karma Kagyu guru is everywhere.
He can be found just outside your front door.
She can be found just inside of it.
Still, it was worthwhile taking the trip because the ability to
remember this crucial point depends upon the guru's magic,
The Karma Kagyu's blessing.
And I would never have realized that Karmapa was not someone else,
Had I not embarked upon the journey.
I am very happy to have finally met Karmama.

2-19-09

Invitation

Come sit under maitri and meditate with me.

If you are a thought, you are welcome.

Come sit under my maitri and meditate with me.

All thoughts are invited, no matter who you are.

If you are a thought about love, please have a seat.

If you are a thought about hate, please feel free to rest your feet.

If you are a thought about sex, it is possible you may vex,

But if you are a thought who is vexed, you are welcome also.

If you are a thought about rage,

You may turn me into a sage,

So please don't apologize for being who you are.

If you would like to be a star,

The dharma doesn't bar

You from passing through my mind.

Why be unkind?

You are equally welcome as all your sister and brother thoughts.

If you are a thought about pride,

You are welcome to come along for the ride.

I will not set you aside or call you evil.

But should I have a thought which is so medieval

That it tries to label you evil,

That medieval thought is just as welcome as you are.

I may have a thought who is a Nazi,*

Or one who is so lazy, it likes to play potsi

All day and night.

I welcome them both without a fight.
I may have a thought that makes no sense.
It requires no defense.
I welcome a thought who likes to sit on the fence,
As well as a thought who takes a stand.
I hope you understand
My meditation instruction.

No thought will be turned away,
Whether you show up night or day.
You may linger if you wish or you may jog through my mind.**
I promise to be kind
To you if you are a thought.
Come sit under maitri and meditate with me.
No thought will be turned away for any reason.
Come sit under maitri and meditate with me.
You are welcome any hour, any season.
If a thought who is a drunken monkey***
Gets into a fight with one who is spunky,
That is fine. Mind can accommodate all sorts of behavior.****
Sometimes my thoughts want to riot.
I just tell them, "Please feel free to try it."
Sometimes my thoughts want to picket.
I say, "Go ahead. I won't issue a ticket."
Some thoughts like to stand on their head,
While others cry and wish they were dead.

I announce, "All you thoughts: feel free to do your own thing.
Maitri will liberation bring.

It is the tree of fruition,

And I never charge rent or tuition

To any thought."

2-21-09

Notes

*Any bigoted thought

**A compulsive thought, for example, is one who lingers.

***Trungpa Rinpoche first used the term "drunken monkey" in his book *Cutting Through Spiritual Materialism* to characterize the nature of samsaric mind.

****This attitude is the exact opposite of the"medical model approach" in which the mind is regarded with suspicion as if it posed a potential threat, and unpleasant or uncomfortable thoughts are treated like enemy soldiers to be stood guard over or gone to war against.

Suicide

Why
Do I want to die
When my world is so good,
All the people so kind,
When my home I did find,
When I live as a warrior
And have learned not to fear my own projections?
Why
Do I want to die,
When I can drink such delicious tea,
When students enjoy classes taught by me?
When they learn
And I can speak clearly and be heard
And am well respected?
When I am soaring like a bird?
It seems so absurd –
This longing for death.
I telephoned a friend in New York.
He told me that I am missed and still loved by all.
I have a comfortable bed to sleep in and plenty of food,
Yet I brood and brood.
My life gets better every day.
Nevertheless, I contemplate ending it.
How can I feel so joyful and so forlorn in the same moment –
One second dancing and singing, the next praying to die?
I dare not cry, lest I lose my breath
Although that is what I long for.

Will the name my Father-Guru gave me,
"Dharma Joy of Enlightenment" ever be actualized
In this dream of a life, or will the dream have to end first?
Although I have been blessed,
I feel cursed by loneliness.
I do not know whether this loneliness will last forever,
Or whether loneliness and joy will find themselves compatible.
I can only take the next step, and then the next
To learn the answer one step at a time.

2-23-09

Loner

I am adequate –
Not lonely at all.
I can stand on my own
And not fall.
I don't need your support,
Don't care for you much.
Don't like your false friendship,
Your icy touch.
Don't need you to stand around me
And click your tongue,
Like I thought I did
When I was foolish and young.
Don't need your false smile
Which is not worth a penny,
And though I seem to be one
And you seem to be many,

I can let you walk by,
Be a minority of one.
I can make my own pleasure
And enjoy my own fun.
If you want to cling to each other,
That is just fine with me,
But you won't hold me down,
I can guarantee.
I will fly like a bird.
I will gallop like a horse.

I will live life fearlessly
And die without remorse.

2-26-09

In-Crowd

I love to chat with a cat
Because I never get into a spat
Like I do with humans.
I never say "no" to a crow
Or ask it "How do you know?"
Since all their pronouncements seem sensible and merit no argument.
I enjoy playing hostess to a monkey
Since the food they eat isn't junky
But bananas are both healthy and delicious.
I get pleasure when I smooch with a pooch.
It is grace when they lick my face
And all of my tension erase.
They teach me to love.
Since humans are vicious for the most part,
It doesn't break my heart
That my most intimate circle of friends consists of all animals.
So if you want to be part of my in-crowd,
You had better grow a tail or you will fail.
Fancy words will be of no avail
In impressing me.

2-28-09

Diamond

(Trungpa and Me)

Once upon a time, there lay a diamond,
Brilliant, sharp and sublime
Buried beneath a sewer,
Covered with feces and grime.
Nobody paid it much notice,
But when the spoke of it, they referred to it as a turd,
And the diamond, not knowing any better,
Believed everything that it heard.
Unaware of its True Nature,
It regarded itself with hate,
And assumed that to be always treated ignobly
And spit on and kicked was its fate.
It said to itself, "Because I am shit,
I deserve a life that stinks."
Thus it found no moment not filled with pain,
No situation not riddled with kinks.
It turned to crime for a living
When it could find no menial jobs.
Though it always felt the impulse to shine,
It held back, stifling itself with sobs.
The diamond thought it needed permission
From someone with a higher degree
To wash itself off and manifest its True Nature,
To sparkle in the world, to just be.
When on occasion, it dared step forward,
The world demanded, "Just who do you think you are?"

That world was a mirror of the diamond's own confusion
Left over from an ancient scar.
Thus this precious, soiled diamond
Did shake instead of shine.
Instead of standing tall,
It always did recline.
Instead of feeling confident,
It lived its life ashamed.
Hiding the true mighty warrior's heart,
It existed small and tamed.

One day, when she was around thirty,
She passed a jewelry store
And glancing into the window,
Saw the finest jewel anyone ever saw.
And though she thought, "I really can't afford much,"
She inquired about the price, just on a self-dare,
But the store clerk answered, with joyful laughter,
"This is yourself you are seeing, my dear."
So the diamond went back home to think that over,
For several decades more,
Each year, washing off just a little more dirt,
To expose a hint of what lay at her core.
And when the illusion of feces was almost all washed away,
And she transformed her sewer into a lovely home,
A beautiful, sparkling diamond disguised as an invisible guru,
Or just a little, invisible bug,
Came crashing right out of her mirror
And gave her a kiss and a hug

Before blowing her house down,
Blowing her house down,
Chasing her out naked into to the world,
To shine, brilliant, sharp and sublime
According to her True Nature.

3-6-09

Space Hooker

When Space sat up in bed, she yawned
And wondered what she would do.
Would she be a wandering vagabond today,
A sumi wrestler or a Buddhist guru.
Then remembered she need not strain her brain,
But based upon last night's dream,
Her day's agenda would simply unfold
By itself, though by choice it might seem.
Now Space was not too enthusiastic,
Since she had had nightmares all night,
And it seemed that a lot of unhappiness
Was in her immediate sight.
So Space was tempted to lie back down
And pull the covers over her head,
But Energy would not allow that behavior
And to him she was wed.

Therefore, Space stood up and stretched.
She wondered what to wear.
She thought she might dress in brown and green,
But Energy demanded, "Try red, my dear."
"Now why not put on those high heeled shoes
Instead of the sneakers you bought?
You may turn out to be someone quite different
Than the professor you thought."
So Space put on a tight red dress
Followed by stiletto heels.

She dressed herself in an identity
Which frightfully terrible feels.
She coined herself *Shady Lady of Tibet,*
A Solely Owned Proprietorship,
Doing Business as Heidi Fleiss, *
To at least feel a little bit hip.
That hipness was in no way a scam.
She was not operating blind,
But understood that it was part of her path
Learning the nature of Mind.
Intelligence was always her nature,
No matter whom she pretended to be,
And all of the labels mere Emptiness.
None a true Me.
Once Space understood this, she felt quite pleased.
In fact, she was overjoyed
At not having to feel inadequate
Or uptight, no matter how she was employed.
She was also thus freed from arrogance
When she wore a high-brow label,
For any idea of being other than Space,
She understood to be a fable.
Now Heidi Fleiss became a guru,
Which was really nothing strange.
Since all forms are Emptiness,
She was never separate from the whole range.

Heidi also became a poet
Thanks to the influence of Energy, her mate.
Then those two, never really separate

Lived out the balance of a challenging, joyous fate.

3-9-09

<u>Note:</u>

*Heidi Fleiss was a madam in Washington, D.C., who ran an up-
scale prostitution ring which serviced all of the senators and other
government bigwigs. The Shady Lady of Tibet was a medieval
Tibetan prostitute who arose in my mind when I practiced as a
prostitute in San Francisco. This medieval, Tibetan "Shady Lady,"
the modern, Jewish Heidi Fleiss and I were all symbols of the same
energy. The understanding of all beings and things in the so-called
"external world" as symbolic rather than truly existent entities in
their own right is known in Vajrayana Buddhism as *Mahamudra*.
Mahamudra practice is especially emphasized in the Karma Kagyu
Lineage.

Part Four:
Europe April 1, 2009 – April 12, 2009

(Decompression)

No One Is An Outsider
(Milarepa in a London Pub)*

This is the House of Zero.

Here sits Nero.

She has forgotten Fearo.

Hope and fear have been flung far away.

This is the practice of No Yana, which never ends.

It protects and defends the Heart.

It is the Mahakala Yana** practiced by me.

No man can practice it.

No man can receive its empowerment.

No man can become it.

There is no man who is equal to me!

Mahakala Yana!

Mahakala Yana!

Mahakala Yana!

Catch me if you can!

Since your ego is quartered in your dick,

I have put a curse on your prick.

Now I am going to cut it off to help you get enlightened.

I am the Vajra Mahakala you have been making offerings to all of

these years,

Praying to for protection from ego's fears,

But it is not you I am here to protect. It is the dharma of truth I defend.

While reciting a dogma of emptiness,

At the same time, you grab on to your penis, like it is going to save you,

Like it is a credential of superiority.

In reality, you have turned it into a credential of inferiority by your worship of it.

Although I am not really here,

I, the Vajra Mahakala, am nevertheless a woman

Who cuts off your precious penis with the blade of a superior mind

And castrates your precious testicles with the Sword of Manjushri.

You kept me isolated all of these years,

Hoping I would go blind from living in the darkness.***

That was very kind

Because instead, it caused me to see the truth of your hypocrisy.

The blindness is yours.

The dharma of truth brings liberation.

In Ultimate Reality, there is no one.

Thus all are equal.

Enlightenment is won by those who love the root guru,

And have been blessed by her or him.

It is not a gift to be bestowed or withheld by any person with a fancy title.

The label "Rinpoche" is as empty as the rest of form's fantasies.

It is only the Heart which frees.

Now I, the Vajra Mahakala, spit upon you,

Thereby slicing apart your ego with the razor of my contempt

Because you think you were born a man with a penis,

You think you are an animal,

You think you are a thing.

If you think you are an object, don't you deserve to be treated like one?

All people, both male and female, are none other than Buddha:

We are unborn.

Our bodies are but intense fantasies which are particularly difficult to
see through.
In your case, unlike my own, it is a fantasy which pays off richly,
Thus making it far more convenient to mouth Absolute Truth than to
live by it.****
I see all you of lamas clearly now,
Licking your lips over the thought of fancy robes and fancy titles,
Patting one another on the back,
And making gifts to each other of phony empowerments
To cover up the truth of your real spiritual impotence.
Since your very superior genitalia
Are the ground for your elevated spiritual standing in ego's delusional
mind and all of its institutions,
Cutting off your balls must be the method of liberation.
Such surgery is the only one which is karmically appropriate and
logical.

Now I, having been locked outside of the walls of your stinking, flea-
ridden monasteries,
Which you have managed to turn against yourselves, making them
into prisons,
Do the real practice of Mahakala which destoys ego,
Having received the one true abhisheka***** which guarantees
liberation in a single lifetime.
Where is the Lineage of Vajradhara? Where is the Heart of Tilopa,
Naropa, Marpa and Milarepa?
It is not found within the monasteries,
For the Lineage of Milarepa has been locked outside of them.
Milarepa has become an outcast in your world.

He neither beats the drum nor blows the horn when the monks all
gather in puja
For you have banished the king of yogins.
Now I, Bird Neshama Trungma, build my own shrine,
And create my own monastery.
I blow my own horn and beat my own drum

For I, Bird Trungma, am not Milarepa's sister.
I, Bird Neshama, am he.
For Chogyam Trungpa was and is Milarepa
The invincible yogin, whose treasure heart
Has been planted in me.

4-3-09
Revised 4/15/09
Revised 7/15/09

Notes

*This poem was actually written in a London pub. The day after
arriving in England, I decided to experiment to find out how
comfortable I would feel as a lay person, so I bought a pair of jeans and
a shirt to change into instead of wearing my robes. Then I went into
a pub and ordered a beer. I finished the beer and ordered a second,
but the bartender refused to serve me, calling me "a fat, ugly dyke." I
told him that if he would not serve me, I would continue to sit where
I was and take up a table, even though it was Saturday evening and the
place was becoming crowded, and that I would remain there until he
either served me my beer or the pub closed, because if he was going to
be rude to me, I would make certain that his misogyny cost him plenty
of money. As the evening progressed, the bartender along with other

men who worked there kept coming to my table and harassing me to force me to leave, asking such questions as "Which mental ward did you just get out of, St. Mary's or St. Frances'?" and telling me to "Go back to the mental hospital, you fat dyke!" This made me think a lot about how the accusation of so-called "menal illness" is used, and about how often words like "schizophrenic," "psychotic" and "mentally ill" are used to control people, women in particular, very similar to the way the word "witch" was used to control and destroy rebellious or non-conformist women in the past. My response was to sit right there at the table and write this poem, while the men stood all around me, hurling these insults. The entire poem was written during this incident in the pub; since I did not leave there from late in the afternoon until the pub closed in the wee hours of the morning, I had plenty of time to sit there and be creative! While I wrote, the bartender and his all-male staff and the Tibetan monks I had just left in India merged in my mind, becoming one big, ugly gang of hideous bigots. This poem was addressed to that gang.

**The path of cutting through ego straightforwardly, without compromise.

***This refers to the segregation and exclusion of women from the monastic system.

****This statement could only be made from the shore of Relative Truth which makes such dualistic distinctions as self and other. Although it is not Absolute Truth, it still does matter; it is never okay to oppress anyone or allow oneself to be oppressed, using Absolute Truth as a justification, saying "What's the difference whom I hurt; we're not real anyway!"

*****spiritual empowerment, usually conveyed during a special, highly ritualized ceremony.

• • •

Recuperation

Sitting outdoors at an Italian café in the City of Westminster,

I sip my coffee with contentment.

I forget to compare it with Asian coffee, which is poison.

I forget to compare it with Nepalese Nescafe and sputter curses.

Just for the present moment, I feel neither agonized nor enraged.

The only true vacation is a mental one.

Having this vacation is a miracle I would never have dared dream of,

let alone pray for.

Long live the Queen!

God save England! God save the Queen!

4-5-09

Starbuck's
Stepping Off the Merry-Go-Round
At the Same Spot That I Stepped On –
(Or Possibly Subtitled Chogyam Trungpa is a
Gentleman Who Always Sees A Lady Home After a Date)

Sitting in a Starbuck's café

In the wealthy and generous city of Geneva, where the people are, on the whole, pleasant in both personality and appearance,

I am already back in New York, although the plane ride is yet two days away.

The offering of lox on a bagel with cream cheese beckons me from behind the counter.

Though I cannot resist the old- time, New York-Jewish fare, I use the situation to practice my French by requesting the *saumon fume*.

Why can't I just relax? Why can't I just bite into it?

I no longer have a home in New York and will be depending upon the generosity of an old friend.

We will see how it goes.

Will I be returning to Dharmasala?

Moving to Boulder?

Renting a too-expensive studio apartment in the Bronx?

I may end my life as a vagabond, although I hope not.

Whatever became of Konchok Yenlak? *

As an old woman named Konchok Yenlakma,

I am anxious to hear.

 My guru is the face of karma.

It is this karma which is my path.

It is this karma which I label a self.

There is nothing else at all.

I have not become a nun, as I was led to believe.

This is not very disappointing for a woman who enjoys getting
dressed up, wearing big earrings and red lipstick.

Just for today, karma and my desire are not at war.

Since whatever I desire, as well as the perception of a self who desires
it, are only karma's manifestations,

Why should there be any conflict at all?

The world is too full of lies and cruelty for me to step forward waving
a white flag.

Nevertheless, just for today, I have lain down my shotgun.

Loving kindness towards my own mind blossoms into compassion for
the world.

Since these are not separate, how could kindness toward myself
not lead to compassion toward a world which only echoes my own
confusion?

The city that used to be my home is now two days away.

Though I can no longer celebrate it as my home,

At least I can courageously bite into my bagel, chew and swallow my
lox.

Cheers to lox with cream cheese on a bagel!

Cheers to blue jeans and also to fancy dresses,

Worn with big earrings and red lipstick and hair to be grown out,

To Washington Heights, Washington Irving High School and
unrequited love in the Washington Square subway station.

Cheers to Lincoln Center and the Metropolitan Opera House in
April 2009, the sixty-third year of my life.

This year, I will celebrate my birthday by attending a performance of
Swan Lake.

Cheers to the swans of Swan Lake – both those who swim in it and those who dance in it, above all else!

4-10-09

Note

*A great yogin and Karma Kagyu lineage holder, who practiced for a long time by wandering alone from place to place.

Part Five:
Back in New York – April to September, 2009

(Living In Judy Hollander's Apartment in Washington Heights)

Delirious Commodes at New York-Presbyterian Hospital

Rich Jew.

Has lots of money in the bank, lots of zeros:

Zero zero zero comma zero zero zero comma zero zero zero point

zero zero.

In this hospital, it is not even enough to purchase a raised toilet seat with,

Not enough for your own commode

Or a roll of toilet paper.

In this hospital, everyone gets the best of care in exchange for the best

of funds

And discrimination is based solely on the size of your bank account.

The color of everyone's money is identical.

Oh, where have all the raised toilet seats gone?

The only way for me to take a piss safely is by standing up.

I take it on the chin. I take it like a man.

Oh, where have all the commodes gone?

I've decided to cut off this verse here.

Believe me, whatever you may be imagining, it was worse.

Since I have had my surgery at this wonderful hospital,

I feel like a male animal

With a lot of testosterone and extra Y chromosomes running wild

around my bedroom.

Was the injection of male hormones the final necessary step to replace

my hip?

If you are on the staff here, you had better watch out

Or I may either throw a punch at you like a man, or butt you like an animal, hard on the ass with my horns.

June 10, 2009

Note

Two days after hip replacement surgery
New York-Presbyterian Hospital
West 168 Street Campus

Burning Down Gyuto Monastery*

I am burning down Gyuto Monastery
While nibbling on an apple and a berry.
As all the texts go up in flames, I will make merry,
But will not chip in His Holiness to bury.
Just throw Karmapa's body to the vultures
And all the worms and creeps of all the different cultures.
I'll chop off the cocks on all the various sculptures
Of Karmapa and his gang of misogynist monks, punks, and morons.
All these phony monastics make me want to puke.
They hide behind their robes as if their robes were their mothers'
skirts,
But what really hurts
Is that they lie about feeling inferior and pretend they are above
others.
These monks avoid and exclude women from their hierarchy not only
because of having soft dicks, but because of having soft brains, which
are addled and foul.
Now I, Bird, have grown into a wise, old owl
With the good karma to not have been born in a man's body in this
life,
Nor battered by the insufferable misery of being the wife
Of some pseudo-religious idiot or mundane merchant with a skinny
brain and a fat testicle.
My mind, which is none other than the shining mind of awakened
Buddhahood,
Is nothing at all.
I am Nothing at all,

156

Still, I am All in being nothing.

These Karma Kagyu monastics regard and treat their nuns as if they were zero,

But the truth is that zero is Nero.

Most monks barely are able to approach or even stand beside those women whom they denigrate,

Let alone excel them in wisdom or knowledge of the dharma.

The only way in which monks are superior to nuns is in being much better at creating phony elevated titles for themselves.

They also excel at tap dancing and patting one another on the back in the hope of receiving fancy-sounding false empowerments.

Now this woman, a former nun who refused to become an adjunct monastic,

Is entirely null and void.

She would only have become an adjunct had she existed.

These very important lamas who regard themselves as wise

May keep their idiot prize: the title "Rinpoche," and the titles "His Holiness," "His Eminence," and so on.

From the point of view of Relative Truth, my advice to these fools is to keep practicing,

Yet if I entertain thinking about them as being real enough to be aggravated by,

That is a certain reminder for me that I must practice what I preach.

June 17, 2009

Note

*His Holiness Karmapa's residence. It is a monastic college – all male students. When I visited there as a nun, I and all the other nuns

were made to sit on the floor, and only the monks were allowed to sit on the low benches. I never imagined anything like this about "my lineage." It turned my world upside down and my guts inside out. His Holiness the Dalai Lama's monastery in McLeod Ganj is sexually segregated as well, as are the other Gelukpa Monasteries, those which belong to the Lineage headed by the Dalai Lama. It is interesting that when His Holiness the Dalai Lama and//or His Holiness Karmapa visit the West, they never give the impression that they've got anything at all like that going on back home, on their own turf. In the West, where women have more rights and are treated with more respect, and where they often are also holding the family checkbooks or their own checkbooks, these very highly evolved dharma masters give no clue whatsoever that while their monks back home are sitting and learning in the monasteries, the nuns are either homeless or are barely surviving without any education by mopping floors for a living by day, while they attempt to study the dharma at night after a day of such miserable labor. The Dalai Lama and His Holiness Karmapa, and the other rinpoches and lamas just come here and smile and smile at everyone, including the moneyed women Buddhists of the West. They are all about love!

Your Face is the Mirror of My Soul
(A Love Poem to the Father-Guru, the Vidyadhara, the Venerable Chogyam Trungpa, Rinpoche)

Your face is the mirror of my soul.

I see myself dancing in your eyes.

Your face is the mirror of my soul,

The portrait of courage who does not compromise

Essence for Appearance.

I bowed to the challenge and accepted the sword you placed into my hand.

Your face is the mirror of my soul.

I knew you to be the Master upon first sight,

Yet recognized myself in the same moment.

Your face is the mirror of my soul,

The mirror of all that exists, of Mind dressed up in the myriad costumes of a Universe.

I read the book of life, birthless and deathless, in your eyes.

You, who are neither a liar nor a hypocrite,

Expose the barbarian hordes. They are not Other.

Though you have always existed in the world fully grown,

Still I feed you milk from my breasts. I feed you all you might need from my bosom.

While you are no child, I nevertheless remain your mother.

Was it not my heart which gave birth to you?

I never loved myself for even an instant before loving you.

Your face is the mirror of my soul.

How can I run away from the battle?

Your face is the mirror of my soul.

You are the warrior riding atop the invisible steed who gallops upon my breath,

The invisible angel who glides in and out,

In and out of me with each breath.

I join with you in holy intercourse to learn that we were never separate from the beginning.

All I had to do was look into my mind by looking at your face,

Which is the mirror of my soul.

7/9/09

To the Vidyadhara, the Venerable Chogyam Trungpa, Rinpoche.

From the moment I first saw you,
You became the reason for my life
And my whole life itself,
Filling me up entirely.
There was no breathe which entered or left my body
Upon which you did not ride,
Upon which you did not dance,
And you made up not only the content of my thoughts,
But inundated every space in between them.
Perhaps that was how I became you.
While the medieval Western word for such magic was "possession,"
The Buddhists of Tibet call it "the transmission of enlightened mind
from teacher to student,"
And those gone beyond think of it in terms of the threefold purity:
No teacher nor student ever existed. No transmission of enlightened
mind ever took place.

I, however, being a very simple person,
Wind up with a headache from so much thinking, so many fancy
words, so much philosophizing.
I step forward, presenting a single word: love.
Then step back.*

You may feel free to psychoanalyze me in your spare time if you wish,

Or create complex theories based upon secret practices whose
instructions are buried under snow mountains or the deepest caverns
of the mind
If you garner enjoyment from it.
I wish you all the best.
I, simple minded woman that I am,
Have given up on trying to figure it all out,
But merely sit home writing poetry in the wee hours of the morning.

7/10/09

Note

*My love for my guru is the only thing which has not changed since
my visit to India – during which I learned such terrible things that I
didn't want to know about. No matter what exalted person betrays
my trust, the guru who lives in my heart will never betray me.

Part Six:
The Poems With Long Blonde Hair

Some Poems Written by Bird Gelman
in 2007 and 2008
(Before shaving her head to become
a nun in September of 2008)

Ari

Ari,

Diamond dealer,

Hot shot.

Flies around the world like nothing, from New York to Johannesburg
to Tel Aviv and back to New York again.

Carries an English textbook on the plane to study verbs en route.

Doesn't care about Shakespeare.

Doesn't care about T.S. Eliot.

Doesn't care about Emily Bronte.

Wants to write better letters to customers

In order to sell more diamonds to get richer.

3-14-07

Cat Girl

My pretty Yentl Flower,
Little gray striped girl,
Sits on my lap on the toilet seat
Letting me stroke her.
She snubs me all of the time,
Except when I'm relieving myself.

3-15-07

Smart Ragemobile

Smart ragemobile

Compact fuse box

Fuses lit by thoughts: think-think-think-think-think.

Kill.

Slam fist through window.

Only previous good karma stops the fuse from exploding just in the nick of time.

Jonathan Swift wrote: "Mankind is a race of the most odious little vermin that nature ever suffered to crawl upon the surface of the earth."

Smart ragemobile agrees.

Compact fuse box says, "Certainly, the poor Irish should sell their babies to be food for the rich. After all, that's just fair and square capitalism, isn't it?"

Think-think-think-think-think.

Rabbi Nachman of Bratslav wrote a story called "The Kingdom of Lies." Of course, it was obvious to all that it was merely a work of fiction.

Think-think-think-think-think.

On Monday mornings, when the businessmen need their workers,

The trains run at rush hour intervals – every two minutes.

Try getting anywhere on Sunday morning to have fun

Without the cash for a taxi in your pocket!

Why is the rich population so small,

While the poor multiply themselves like rabbits?

You can never be too rich or too thin,

But when you're exhausted from a day of tedious work,
You bring home Kentucky Fried Chicken.
Charity in this country is a penny and a spit.
First they put a penny in your hand and then they spit in it.
Since I am late for work, I should write a note to my supervisor
explaining the reason.
But the trouble is, I only know how to write in English
And the Chairman of the English Department is not quite proficient
in reading that language yet.

But why be prejudiced?
Why feel angry?
Isn't it all about love?
Lovey-lovey-lovey-lovey-dovey.
If I had the money, I would go away on a spiritual retreat
And become an enlightened holy yogini
But since I am poor and cannot afford to pay the guru,
I must remain a barbarian digging ditches.
Nevertheless, if I have the guru's love,
I will be a blessed barbarian and find treasures in my digging.
Dig-dig-dig-dig-dig.
Think-think-think-think-think.
Smart Ragemobile would surely blow her brains out
Were it not for curiosity about where all the thoughts-thoughts-
thoughts will lead her.

March 18, 2007

In Praise of Fancy Titles

She steps into the doorway of the college where she teaches,

And the guard says, "Good morning, Professor."

She enters the office to pick up her roster,

And the secretary says, "Good morning, Professor."

In her classroom, the errant student says, "I forgot my homework,

Professor. I promise I'll bring it in next week";

The not-so-bright student says, "What was that homework again,

Professor?";

And the best student says, "Professor, I interpreted that soliloquy."

She is professor – professor – professor.

Her pay is maximum ego and minimum wage.

Perhaps one of her students, who is a hot shot on Wall Street

Will employ her as his secretary for the summer.

If not, perhaps she will qualify for food stamps.

March 19, 2007

Little Levity

Keep off the sugar, Sugar!

If you want to live like a queen, stay away from nicotine!

And don't drink booze unless you want to lose!

Semester's over.

I'll take a vacation in Dover.

6-07

Sister

I.

I have a picture of her holding a book with the title *Lassie* on the
cover.

Father told her to pose that way.

"Pose like a typical little girl. Turn cover reading *Lassie* toward
camera."

"Such a sweet child!" say the picture's viewers. "Such an adorable
little girl!"

Where were you inside when you posed for that picture?

Was that a spirit smiling, or a face's necessary ritual?

I didn't know there was somebody home, hidden behind the Lassie
smile.

I didn't know there was a sister to love or a self to do the loving.

We were two zombies.

Bodies with minds cut off, going through rituals:

Everything is fine. Everything is perfect.

Mindlessness necessary to survive,

Pretending the nightmare hadn't caught and enslaved us,

Pretending the horror wasn't going on all around.

I didn't realize you were acting, because understanding you would
have cracked open my own shell. I was afraid it would destroy me.

It was necessary to pretend you were a thing:

There is no real sister here requiring love, compassion, crying to be
known.

Get along.

Don't fight too much.

Above all, don't scratch beneath the surface.
Be careful, or Lassie-girl may bleed,
And then we will both die.
Two zombies who could have been sisters never touched or made contact.
I never knew my sister.

2.

We were both terror-struck, caught in the nightmare.
Our souls were petrified, unable to reach out, to even think of having a life,
Although we dreamed of it.
Living with parents, both of whom were insane,
Anything could happen to us,
Anything could be done to us.
Karma placed us in a love-free household, headed by madmen.
Grandpa and grandma were dead by the time you came around.
For me, they were my anchor, my hope,
Some stability – sanity – to grasp on to.
That anchor was not there for you.
Your terror was pure, unmitigated.
You turned to ultraorthodoxy to be your anchor.
You got married and had babies – seven – one after the other,
Trying to make that husband ad those babies be for you what grandpa and grandma had been for me:
A port of safety,
A port of sanity,
A haven from the nightmare that pervaded us.
Your effort failed because the hauntedness was frozen inside you,
cutting you off from that chosen family.

Their love was unable to penetrate your frozen wall.

It was not your fault.

Now we have to look, you and I, and notice ourselves. Feelings will no longer result in destruction.

Max and Lillian are dead.

We are safe now, little sister.

We can look inside ourselves,

Look inside each other.

We don't have to be zombies anymore.

We can knock on each other's door

And find somebody home.

3.

I keep constructing the golden calf over and over again.

Each encounter with the Holy surprises me.

"What? You're still here?

What? You haven't betrayed me?

You still love me? You haven't changed your mind?

You haven't melted and metamorphosized into something less?

Into a brass token?"

I keep trying to melt down my earrings,

But the Truth is shinier than the brightest, shiniest gold.

Since you are infinite and omnipresent, which includes being inside of me,

I don't need a golden calf,

But how can I expand my feeble brain which keeps forgetting you?

Maybe in some future state,

I will finally learn to trust.

6-4-07

Mirror*

To the Holy Father Guru:
If I had feathers to spread
As beautiful as the peacocks'
And spread them wide before your raised seat,
If I had the wings of an eagle
And soared with an eagle's grace through the heavens to your rainbow palace,
Or if I came as a cripple, limbs twisted, back bent, to offer myself before your throne,
Still, I could not declare your glory as fully as you deserve.
The proud peacock, colorful feathers displayed, declares "The Father Guru is King."
The roaring eagle, flying gracefully among the clouds, exclaims, "He is holy."
The cripple intones, "Remember, remember, Mind and the Guru are one."
When I play my own sonata,
When I sing my own composition,
When I dance my dance,
Write my verse,
Paint my landscape,
Sculpt my statue,
It is yours.
It is yours also
When I cook my meal and eat dinner.
The Father Guru's mandala is a mirror
In which everything reflects only Mind-essence.

The world is none other than Mind-essence,
And I am thick with you.

7/23/07

Note

*This is what I call a "converted poem" or a "poem that shaved its head." It was originally written to God – not Father Guru, and is written very much in Torah style of high praise for the holy. It was later edited into what I considered to be a "Buddhistly correct" poem.

Impressions – Portraits of Mind*

1.

Speaker at Debtors' Anonymous Meeting:

"I did this. I did that. I got this. I got that. I want this. Then I want that. I've got special credentials. My body and my ego are huge. I'm a giant son-of-a-bitch; I'm Somebody – a big, ugly fucker. Kneel down and worship me."

Couple on Train on Way Home from Debtors' Anonymous Meeting:

"We're so poor. Look how beaten down we are. Life sucks. We're sucky life's losers."
Sad looking round-eyed woman: "Living in this world is such a burden." Man (sitting with hands cupped in front of his genitals): "Don't beat me, Mr. Prison Guard. Please don't beat me. I lose. I'm a loser. I admit it. I give up. Please don't hit me again."

Man and woman meant for each other. A Perfect Couple. (They call this love).

Number One: Big, ugly, fucker ego.
Number Two: Helpless losers. Ego twisted to look like Not-ego.
Their message to the Universe: We are dirt.

2.

What does it make *me* then if I hate all of the portraits of Mind I see?

An evil spirit? A ruthless ruffian? A poetic punk?

A cold coward too scared to love my own perversity with the passion it deserves?

Can I feel the compassion these misshapen creatures want to give rise to in me and live,

Or will my ceaseless tears cover me over and dissolve me?

Might that amount of pain and love be a fatal combination that moves me out of bounds, off the craggy, slanted playing field?

All of us are broken.

We are people belly crawling through the primordial waters of the world, trying to stay afloat just long enough to grab on to the next tiny island.

We live in a nightmare. We hold on to the superstition, mistaking it for real.

The only one here is the Sovereign, riding a train home from a Debtors' Anonymous meeting, pretending to be a convict and a woman and a big, ugly, fucker ego.

The Mind is not bound. It's nature is free and needs not be liberated.

Buddha is awake without nightmares.

October 21, 2007

_____

Note

*Another poem edited to be "Buddhistly correct." It was originally entitled "Portraits of the King," with the term King referring to God. The words Mind and Buddha in the last stanza were also changed from the original word, which was "God." Since the Father-Guru has acted as God in my life, these two terms are synonymous to me, for all practical purposes. Despite my understanding of my inseparability from or oneness with or sameness as the the root

guru (God) - (Emptiness, no matter what costume it wears, is still Emptiness), my relationship to him as one which is filled with awe, love and wonder, remains unchanged and unchangeable.

Sugar

Exhaustion is excuse to grab sugar.

A food diaspora: where we eat without self-respect.

Stuff anything into the mouth to keep the kid quiet.

Make aliyah: Move up to vegetables!

God was in this house, but I didn't know it.

I get all puffed up from eating sugar, God says.

Feed me with honor. I am a high class person.

My Father-Mother is the Divine.

Spare me from cheap, icing thrills.

I should keep Shabbos,

Avoid eating shrimp, pork, and sugar,

Keep a stiff upper lip and a straight spine.

But God, I am so exhausted,

And fall always, always way below the mark.

Were Divine Justice the sole determinant of my future,

I would never emerge from the misery pit.

But You, God, add compassion to the karma stew,

Allowing me to lift up my head, breath, gaze at the mountain tops,

Leaping from summit to summit across their eternal range

To the Angel of Redemption's joyful melodies.

1-7-08

Note

Ibid

Rage-aholic Transgender

When I die, I may come to heaven fighting and cursing all the way.
The divine angels may have to hold me down. I may smash my fist
through the pearly gate. If I do that, will I bleed?
This girly-girl is one heck of a masculine guy.
Maybe that was why
I hated my father so and wanted him to die.
He could be on the outside that which I had to keep inside,
And could show what I could only hide.*
I am the hellish father
And the heavenly one too.
My lover,
And he whom I despise.
And God did the act of tsimtsum**in order to love himself.
And God did the act of tsimtsum in order to hate himself.
And God did the act of tsimtsum in order to be a self.
Genesis is choiceless.
How can a Creator not create?
I am; therefore, I am.
I am not. Am I not?
What is going on here is more amazing than anything formerly
suspected.
Out of nothing, something cannot be born
Nor exist.
I am neither Eyn Sof*** nor the writer of this poem
Which has never been written.
If I am tired
And fall into bed tonight,

It is only due to ignorance.
Still, I am sorry to see
That my beloved daughter
Is a rage-aholic.****

January 20, 2008

Notes

*I thought about the possible multiple meanings of this long after it was written.

**tsimtsum – (Hebrew) contraction

***Eyn Sof – (Hebrew) Nothingness (*There is not a thing*), regarded as an aspect of God in the Jewish tradition. This is similar to the Buddhist *dharmakaya*.

****Father-Guru (Father God) implicitly speaking here.

Kissing Cellular Guru Goodnight*

Dear Guru,
You're in my essence,
My spinal fluid,
My saliva,
All of the tiniest nuclei of my smallest cells.
How can you be somewhere called there,
And I be somewhere different called here?
I have no essence,
No spinal fluid,
No saliva,
No cells.
All of the Nothing going on here is fascinating though.
What is the Guru?
What is my heart?
What the longing?
In the beginning was the word *the*
Thus, all of this came into being,
The Holy Mystery metamorphosized into matter,
Mind into flesh.
Yet there was none.
Still, you, my only Father-Guru,
Exist in the reality of my life.
So in my mind's eye, I see myself kissing you on the cheek good night.

Good night.

March 9, 2008

Note

*Originally "Kissing Cellular Deity Goodnight"

181

A Tear in the Fabric: Day Pass

Ouch! Caught in the net again.
Alright. So it's time for another lesson.*
I swallow bitterness.
Your medicine makes whole.
This delusion of mine
Of a sick, broken world
Makes me sick and broken,
Creates crippled dream.
The magnitude of the hallucination is so immense
This schizophrenia ward ever expanding,
Creating obsession of time – space – universe
Upheld by the Mind of mind.

Is there a Dreamer?
A Net Weaver?
A Creator of the Hologram?
Holygram?

I do not have any answers,
Only questions.
Knowing this is the first step toward sanity,
Toward finding the hidden doorway out.

April 10, 2008

Note

*Another reincarnation (or another dream with its set of
hallucinations), depending upon your point of view.

A Walk in Fort Tryon Park Shortly Before Dusk

Quiet mind is mind of vision.

Shouting mind closes my eyes.

In my silent inner space, image of tree wearing pink leaves for a hat

Is Mind's beautiful feminine face adorned with pastel ribbons.

Adolescent boys ride past on bicycles yelling curses at one another.

They mirror my own forgetfulness.

I am brought back from confused delirium by chirping soprano voices,

A chorus of avian brethren, who are the bodies and voices of Awareness

Projected in an illusory outward direction.

There really is no center point.

Birds grow silent as the sun lowers its bright golden head downward past the horizon

To rest on the water.

The sonorous sparkling universe dances its ballet dance

While I carefully note all of this as a distinct, individual observer

Who exists only in my imagination.

April 15, 2008

Messiah Cometh*

Messiah cometh
On a day when the skies are filled with music, and the air envelopes earth in her soft breathing.
Messiah cometh
On a day when space quivers and its undulating energy dances a dance of innocent, seductive glee.
Messiah cometh.
The birds herald her, chirping her name, gliding through the air, wings outspread in adulation, happiness liberated from inside their tiny bird bellies and throats.
Their chirping is like laughter.
Out of my heart, a bird song bellows forth.
When Messiah cometh,
All walls and all barriers, both visible and invisible, will melt instantaneously
Turning into flowing, liquid silk.
When Messiah cometh
There will no longer be any you and I to separate us from one another or from holiness.

Permeable laughing lambs leap inside the caves of penetrable majestic mountains.
The lambs can enter and leave them in the blink of an eye, in the instant it takes for a thought of them to arise and fall.
A magical tigress nurses her cubs atop Mt. Sinai
Giving forth milk eagerly. She knows her and her cubs' True Nature.
When Messiah cometh

We finally understand all of the answers to all of the questions.

When Messiah cometh

Peace does a somersault.

The cripple does a somersault and pain forgets to cry out.

There is no liberation where slavery does not exist.

Death is vanquished when delusion of finite substantiality is
overcome.

When Messiah cometh,

Fear is no longer remembered.

When Messiah cometh,

Heaven is everywhere

And no one is separated from heaven or from herself ever again.

When Messiah cometh,

No creature is hungry, angry, lonely or tired anymore.

May, 2008.

Note

*I started spontaneously hearing the words for this poem in my mind
as I was listening to a recording of Rabbi Shlomo Carlebach singing
the Hebrew prayer song "Micha Mocha," so I just grabbed a pen in a
hurry.

Part Seven:
Two Essays

The Misinterpretation of Karma as Psychopathology: An Essay Addressed to Buddhist-Oriented Mental Health Professionals and Others

By Ani Jangchup Peta Paldren Chokyi
(Bird Trungma)

When I was in my early thirties, I became inspired to become a nun in the Karma Kagyu Lineage of Tibetan Buddhism. I traveled to Boulder, Colorado, where my guru, Chogyam Trungpa, Rinpoche, lived in order to seek his blessing and assistance. At that time, he refused to help me become a nun, although I am certain that he did grant his blessing. I began a fast in order to prove to him that I was a "worthy candidate" to become a nun, and I fasted down to 43 pounds before that situation ended. A short while later, I found myself in San Francisco as a prostitute. This was neither a "free will" decision, nor was it the result of any kind of "disordered thinking." It was something I was compelled to do by the "guru who lived in my mind," in spite of my most ardent attempts to avoid it. One attempt involved pouring acid all over my face and body, because I reasoned that if I were scarred, I would become "unsaleable." However, the acid did not leave a single mark anywhere on me. In another attempt to avoid the inevitable, I turned to the nearby municipal mental health clinic and told the psychiatrist there that I was hallucinating. "I am being ordered to become a prostitute," I told him, "and I am afraid I will not be able to stop myself. Please help me." The psychiatrist helped me by prescribing Thorazine. The medication was so effective in cutting my anxiety level that it enabled me to obey the difficult command, which I had up until then been unable to carry out because it triggered too much fear. I swallowed 50 mg of Thorazine, and an hour later, stepped out on to Mission Street to turn my first trick. That was a very successful psychiatric intervention!

This "Trungpa within" was neither exactly real, nor was he a hallucination, as the term is ordinarily understood. For one thing, I never perceived any commands coming from outside myself. I was not "hearing voices." Instead, the command was generated from within. I found the words "I want to become a prostitute" going through my mind, even though I knew for certain that I had no such desire. I also sensed the words being "thought of," not by my own personality, but by "Trungpa's." I even felt like they were being thought with a Tibetan accent and intonation! A few years earlier, I had been told by the nun Pema Chodron, "The guru cannot change your karma, but he can speed it up, so you go through it and it comes to an end more quickly." In other words, the guru can help you to live out in one lifetime what it might ordinarily take many lifetimes to go through. This "emptying out" of karma is what is meant by the Buddhist term *liberation*. Now the "internal guru" was holding a gun to my head, forcing me to do what I had to do. Trungpa's face and voice were the face and voice of karma. I didn't understand this at the time, though. When I later returned to New York, the city of my birth, pregnant and with syphilis, I committed myself to a mental hospital. I was schizophrenic, they told me. Soon I was discharged to sit home swallowing more pills.

There were several more so-called "psychotic episodes" after that, each one triggered by the "Trungpa within." In 2002, "he" insisted that I quit my job in New York and take off on the spot for Nova Scotia in order to join Gampo Abbey, the Buddhist abbey there. I knew full well it didn't make any sense, since an application and meditation instructor's recommendation were required. As I boarded the plane in New York, after having thrown away all of my credit cards at "the guru's insistence," I was completely aware that I had no chance of success whatsoever in joining the abbey. When I inevitably became stranded in Halifax without money for the plane ride home, I telephoned a rabbi friend in New York and told him "I've been hallucinating." I didn't believe that was true, but I was desperate to get home. He arranged for my transport back to New York and subsequent admission to Gracie Square Hospital.

Another time, "Trungpa commanded" that I leave my apartment and go downstairs to the lobby of my co-op naked. When the police arrived, their remarks were cruel and arrogant, so I refused to speak to them or cooperate in any way. They carried me into the ambulance because I refused to walk. When I arrived at the Psychiatric Emergency Room of Columbia-Presbyterian Hospital, I sensed the nurses' contempt for "another mental case" and refused to cooperate with them as well by participating in any kind of interview. A few days later, after I awoke from my Haldol slumber, the doctor informed me that I had been catatonic. Catatonic my eye! It was just too painful to go along with being demeaned and treated like an inferior once again. Therefore, I decided – as Nancy Reagan put it so well – to "just say No." My non-cooperation policy was translated by the hospital staff as catatonia.

In spite of these "episodes" (or more likely, because of them), I eventually evolved the kind of life-style I had long wished for. I was a very late bloomer. Since my teens, I had dreamed of being an English teacher; it was not until I was in my late fifties that I began teaching expository writing at an urban college. In my early sixties, I started writing myself. I had always believed since childhood that I would become a writer. I started writing poetry, as well as a memoir which included all my experiences as a Buddhist. Obviously, much of it was about Trungpa. Before I was halfway through, I realized that "he was co-authoring it." I got as far as page 650 before "he stepped off the pages of the manuscript" and forced me to throw both it and my computer down the incinerator. I resigned from my teaching position, sold my apartment, and was "escorted by him" to Nepal, to seek ordination as a nun from his dharma brother, Karma Kagyu guru Thrangu Rinpoche.

It was not that I was ever "a bad girl" during all of those years after I left Boulder. I never stopped taking medication until the last year. Though my prescription was changed several times, all of the pills were like candy. They never had any effect on me whatsoever.

Karma is karma.

I paid for the best psychotherapy. I participated in psychodrama and attended individual counseling sessions. The psychodrama group was wonderful and helped me to mature artistically and socially. However, it did not prevent me from throwing away my computer and traveling to Nepal.

Karma is karma.

I have been practicing meditation in Kathmandu under the guidance of Thrangu Rinpoche since October 2008. What I have learned is that I and the world in which I exist are both karmically-induced illusions. Nevertheless, these illusions are the reality within which I must live. I am determined to live fully, with my head held high.

There is nothing wrong with me now, nor has there ever been. I do not have a so-called "schizophrenic personality" -- I am not childish and am certainly in no way docile. Right from the beginning, the patronizing attitudes of all the mental health workers enraged and sickened me, because I was not sick.

That which you mislabel psychopathology is nothing other than karma. That is the reason why, despite your best efforts, most of your patients never change. That is the reason why individuals spend their entire adult lives sitting in day care centers, attending weekly counseling sessions and discussing and discussing and discussing the same problems and the same case histories over and over again, ad nauseum. That is the reason why people in their 60's and 70's still sit banging their heads against the wall, bemoaning the abuses heaped upon them by their mothers when they were three years old. That is the reason for the infamous revolving door of mental institutions.

Your approach is to try to protect your patients from their minds.

The whole world is nothing other than mind. How can you protect them?

What you term "mental illness" and what I call "karma" are really nothing other than immaturity, the inabililty to grow up. People run to therapists to be their mommies and daddies – to hold their hands and solve their problems for them and tell them that everything will be alright. They go to hospitals to be taken care of like little children.

The cure for one's life is not swallowing a pill, and it is not running to some ostensibly "powerful other" to be saved. The only cure is to grow up. The truth is that everything will *not* be alright unless one does the karmic work necessary to make it so.

My parents were extremely deficient in their child rearing skills, which in the long run, turned out to be beneficial. When I moved out of their house at the age of 21 to travel across the country to California, the sum of my life skills was limited to brushing my teeth and buttoning my coat. I came to Buddhism and to Trungpa's organization, Vajradhatu, not long after arriving in California. I was clueless about life. I suffered from a kind of profound idiocy that could easily be misinterpreted as pathological.

Since then, I have pursued a path of hard knocks. This was not something I volunteered for. Yet it is true that I asked Trungpa for his help, and that I offered him my body, speech and mind. The vajrayana tradition of samaya bondage is real. The term "bondage" is not metaphoric.

Obviously, I have not been alone and entirely unprotected in the karmic shark tank. I am alive today, more than thirty years after having met Trungpa, with a sharp and lucid mind. I am able to share my thoughts and experiences with others, and I am only too happy to do so.

At a seminar in Los Angeles I attended in the late 1970's, Trungpa played with the mantra contained in the Buddhist *Heart Sutra* that goes "Om gate, gate, paragate, parasamgate, bodhi svaha" by restating it as "Om grow up svaha." Perhaps many of the students who heard him that day thought it was just a cute little joke. It was no cute joke. That is the heart of the Buddhist path. It is the heart of what life is about. There is no difference. You can use a lot of fancy, esoteric terms if you wish. You can use a lot of professional sounding, pseudointellectual jargon. It boils down to the same thing: you've got to be willing to do the work and stop playing it safe. That is the only path to psychological – spiritual adulthood. As therapists, you've got to be willing to stop protecting your patients, keeping them safe and snug like an infant in a crib. Obviously, you've got to stop living that way yourselves.

Quit saying "tut tut tut" and feeling sorry for people. It doesn't help them. It just makes them worse. One cannot run away from karma. One cannot avoid one's life. The idea we have all been fed that life is supposed to be easy is misinformation.

So don't be a jerk,
And do your work.
Om grow up svaha.

1-15-09

Global Warming: A Proposal to Create a Team to Change the Theme of the Dream From a Planet Heating Up to a Planet Cooling Down*

By Ani Jangchup Peta Paldren Chokyi
(Bird Neshama Trungma)

In Tibetan Buddhism, the Kadampa slogan "All dharmas should be regarded as dreams" reminds us to not take things as being solid or absolutely real. This life we live is like a dream. Obviously then, the same holds true for our world. Nothing about our world is a hard fact. Its appearance is not absolute truth. Nevertheless, we would be foolish to think that our lives or our world do not matter because they are not absolutely real. Our lives matter, and we want to live in the most dynamic and genuine way that we can. Our world matters because, whether or not it is absolutely real, it is the only world we have to live in. We want to fill our lives and our world with goodness. Therefore, we have to preserve our beautiful and fragile planet, covered with tall green trees and with snow-covered mountains and with life-sustaining, refreshing waters. We have to lovingly care for our diverse population of handsome, wild animals, so delightful and funny and interesting to watch and to learn about. They are our neighbors, with whom we share this turf, this planet which we call our home. It is not just a matter of doing social work for others, or "joining the Red Cross," as Trungpa, Rinpoche sometimes used to put it. Our tender, loving care must be extended to all, even from a so-called "selfish" standpoint. Both the Buddhadharma and modern physics teach us that at the core of what is, there is no duality. From the time I was a small child, I have always loved animals, and since I have begun practicing meditation, I have come to understand that those animals which I love so much are projections of my own True Nature, which includes fearlessness, innocence and beauty. The deep affection I have always felt for animals cannot be separated from my own self-love and self-respect. I am impelled, therefore, to do whatever I can to see to it that they, and we, all thrive together.

Neither the animals nor the humans are thriving at this time. As our planet grows hotter and hotter, polar bears are drowning en masse, because the ice islands they depend upon for a rest when they swim are melting faster and faster. They are being forced to keep swimming until exhausted, they go down. What an awful way to die! True, there is neither birth nor death; they are illusions. Try explaining that to a terrified bear though, as it gasps for its last breaths of air, or explain it to a confused and frightened penguin as the ice cracks underneath its feet. Of course, there is no real *they*, no such group as *them*. Yes, I understand that. No, it doesn't help me sleep any better at night. Argument number two: if it is alright to ignore the plight of the polar bears, because it is all just a dream anyway, then maybe it is okay for women in the dharma to be treated as second class citizens on that same basis. Why bother integrating the monasteries or having any women rinpoches ? Just keep letting the nuns come in during the day to mop the floors! (And the" very intelligent," educated, wealthy, Western lay women to come in for private interviews with the all-male rinpoches and write big checks made out to those very same monasteries which bar women from living in them and participating in all of their benefits, such as the receipt of a first rate Buddhist education and the privileges that come along with that. These Western women don't seem to think about it too much. After all, they are getting private interviews with the gurus, right? They are special! Who gives a darn about those stupid Tibetan nuns anyway!)

Say, I once heard that the Buddhadharma had something or other to do with cutting through ego. It must have been my mistake!

But I digress! Forgive me.

One of Thrangu, Rinpoche's monks once asked me whether, in my opinion, Relative Truth matters at all. Right on the spot, I answered yes, but later, I went home and thought about it and thought about it and thought about it some more, because I wasn't certain whether or not I had answered his question correctly.

Now a half year later, my answer is still yes. It is true that form is emptiness. On the other hand, though, the Heart Sutra also teaches us that "Emptiness also is form. Emptiness is no other than form." * So if you want to discount form, saying it is somehow inferior to emptiness, you cannot. Which is the same thing as saying that if you want to discount Relative Truth, saying it is inferior to Absolute Truth, you cannot do that either.

Why not?

Because, according to the Heart Sutra, they are the same! Since form is emptiness, then what we are calling "Relative Truth" is really the same as Absolute Truth.

Here is a good way of looking at it: Absolute Truth expresses itself through Relative Truth.

The idea that there are two separate truths is a myth – (or maybe just a handy teaching device).

So – to get down to the main point of this essay – the dharma does not provide us with any excuse to mistreat anyone or to ignore anyone's suffering. Please, whoever you are, no matter what important title you hold, do not misuse the dharma in this way. If you want to be cruel or arrogant or abuse or ignore anyone, go find yourself some other alibi; don't use the dharma!

• • •

Our beautiful world was seen as the human realm of *Jambudvipa* by traditional Buddhists. It was a good place for humans to practice the dharma, work, raise families, grow old, eventually become enlightened. Mt. Meru was in the center. Though Jambudvipa was no paradise, it was also no hell realm.

As earth continues to heat up, it is turning into a hell realm. If we allow this to happen, perhaps the hell realm is where we belong.

More and more animal species are disappearing from the planet every day.

More and more once fertile land is being stricken by draught. The whole earth is changing, turning into a desert.

Human beings are developing bizarre, new diseases created by the change in weather. Plants and trees are becoming sick and are dying. The animals who feed off them will become sick and die too. The humans who eat the sick animals will be doomed.

As we have already shown, Nothing *does* matter. Therefore, I would like to put forth the following proposition: that as Buddhists, we work together to create a Team to Change the Theme of the Dream From a Planet Heating Up to a Planet Cooling Down. Our mode of operation would not be marching on picket lines or organizing demonstrations. Instead, we will cool down the planet by doing *directed tanglen* practice. We will each take ten minutes of every sitting meditation period to breathe in the heat and pollution of earth and then breathe out our own cool freshness into the atmosphere. If enough of us do this, we can have a real impact upon the temperature of the world (a world which exists only in a dream). We should understand that this is possible, *not in spite* of the fact that nothing exists outside of mind, but precisely *because of it.* Since there is nothing "objectively out there" there is nothing which could be impervious to mind's actions.

I further propose that all Buddhist organizations everywhere in the world make this *directed tanglen* a regular part of their practices. All Buddhist teachers and leaders should instruct their disciples to do this practice, and the commitment to do *directed tanglen* should be incorporated into every Refuge and Bodhisattva vow ceremony. Finally, every Buddhist should request his or her family members and friends to do the practice daily. Obviously, all of these actions need to be taken immediately.

As Buddhists, we always say that the way to heal the ills of the world is to work with our own minds. Now is the time for us to practice what we preach, and to demonstrate to the world, once and for all, that this idea makes sense and is the most effective way to change things for the better. All it requires on our parts is a little investment of time. Besides saving precious lives, which is our primary purpose, our success as a Team in Changing the Theme of the Dream From a Planet Heating Up to a Planet Cooling Down would bring great credit to the Buddha's teachings and encourage many people, who are now non-Buddhists, to practice the Buddhist path.

Originally written 10/08
Revised 2/09
Revised 9/09

*The "Heart Sutra" is a text which is recited daily by many Buddhists. It is part of a group of teachings known as the *Prajnaparamita* teachings, meaning teachings of transcendent intelligence.

Breinigsville, PA USA
08 October 2009
225470BV00002B/23/P